D1736157

USES FOR JOURNAL KEEPING

AN ETHNOGRAPHY OF WRITING IN A UNIVERSITY SCIENCE CLASS

Writing Research
Multidisciplinary Inquiries into the Nature of Writing

edited by Marcia Farr,
University of Illinois at Chicago

USES FOR JOURNAL KEEPING

AN ETHNOGRAPHY OF WRITING IN A UNIVERSITY SCIENCE CLASS

BY

ANNE C. JOHNSTONE

REVISED AND EDITED BY

BARBARA JOHNSTONE

AND

VALERIE BALESTER

ABLEX PUBLISHING CORPORATION
NORWOOD, NEW JERSEY

Printed in the United States of America

Library of Congress Cataloging-in-Publication Data

Johnstone, Anne C.
    Uses for journal keeping: an ethnography of writing in a university science class / by Anne C. Johnstone. — Rev. and edited by Barbara Johnstone and Valerie Balester.
        p.   cm. — (Writing research)
    Includes bibliographical references (p.) and index.
    ISBN 0-89391-888-1. — ISBN 1-56750-052-8 (pbk.). —

    1. English language—Scientific English—Study and teaching—Social aspects.   2. English language—Rhetoric—Study and teaching—Social aspects.   3. Science—Study and teaching (Higher)—Social aspects.   4. Diaries—Authorship—Social aspects.   I. Johnstone, Barbara.   II. Balester, Valerie M.   III. Title.   IV. Series: Writing research (Norwood, N.J.)
PE1475.J55   1994
808'.042'071173—dc20   94-9942
                                                                          CIP

Ablex Publishing Corporation
355 Chestnut Street
Norwood, New Jersey 07648

FOR VINCENT MILOT

CONTENTS

EDITORS' PREFACE

As much as we have enjoyed working on this project, we wish that we had not had the opportunity to do so. Anne Johnstone completed this study in 1988, a year before her death, at 35, in a bicycling accident. Barbara Johnstone, a linguist, is her sister; Valerie Balester, a rhetorician, is a colleague of Barbara's. Discussing and critiquing the study as it was being written, in Barbara Johnstone's case, and reading it afterwards, in Valerie Balester's, convinced us that it was worth bringing to publication. We found it novel, compelling, and beautifully written.

In preparing this book, we worked with material hastily gathered at the time of Anne Johnstone's death: her manuscript, a conference paper based on part of it, some of her notes, transcripts of some of her research interviews, and several other bits and pieces. We had no intention of reanalyzing the data or making new claims about it, and we have not done so. The research on which the study is based, and the conclusions drawn from it, are entirely the author's. Our role has been editorial, and has consisted in doing what was necessary to turn a doctoral dissertation written for a small audience into a book for a larger one. We have done a fair amount of rearranging and a little stylistic editing. We have added some material that clarifies connections between this study and the concerns of its potential readers, particularly as the study relates to writing across the curriculum, and we have supplemented the discussion in places with extra examples. We hope that the result appears seamless.

Our greatest debt is to each other, for having faith that this project was worth doing and for teaching each other a great deal about collaborative editing. We are also grateful to Marcia Farr, to Joanne Palmer at Ablex, and to an anonymous reader of the manuscript. Barbara Johnstone's energy was sustained during the project by Io, Valerie Balester's by Spiros Vellas. This book is dedicated to Vincent Milot, who did more than anyone else to sustain Anne Johnstone's energy while she was writing it.

AUTHOR'S ACKNOWLEDGMENTS

This brief paragraph inadequately conveys my thanks for the time, energy, and interest that many people gave to this project. They include the participants in "Spaceship Earth" in the summer of 1986, who made this study possible; the members of my doctoral advisory committee at SUNY Albany, and particularly Steve North, who helped me make it thorough and coherent; the members of my unofficial advisory committee, particularly Barbara Johnstone and Vincent Milot, who helped me understand what I was writing; and other equally invaluable friends and supporters at the University of Northern Iowa Center for Academic Achievement. I also thank Jo Sindlinger and Pat Godwin for excellent transcribing and typing help, and Todd Andrews and Meg Seckendorf for logistical support. As a condition of their participation in this study, my informants were guaranteed anonymity. Accordingly, their names have been changed.

1

JOURNAL WRITING AS A SOCIOPOLITICAL PROCESS

Exponential growth—whew! The principle seems too easy which translates into I'll mess up, bet ya. Wonder why coal heat feels warmer than other heating methods? There are so many facts about coal deposits I never knew. I wonder what I was doing back in geography class. People already getting excited about tomorrows debate!

This entry from a student's journal was written at the beginning of the final week of a four-week summer-session introductory geology course. Beth had been struggling to get caught up in her reading for this course. She had enrolled in the course partly for the general education credit it would earn her; partly because, having grown up in farm country, she was interested in environmental geology issues; and partly because what she learned about these issues was material for conversation with Lonnie, a man she liked who was taking a more advanced geology course and who made the 2 1/2-hour round-trip commute to campus with her each day. Beth wrote this entry as Lonnie drove her from campus to the country club where she worked a forty hour week as a cook. That day her professor, Carl Weber, had lectured to his class on petroleum energy sources and on the population growth curve of energy consumers.

Let's suppose that we wanted to describe Beth's purposes in writing this entry as she did, and we had to guide us only the text of the entry, Professor Weber's written description of the journal assignment, and what the literature on journal keeping would tell us. We would see the features of expressive rhetoric that Britton, Fulwiler, and others have delineated—first-person pronouns, colloquial diction, informal punctuation—and we would hear the rhythms of everyday speech (Fulwiler, 1987). We might be likely to say that Beth used this entry to express bafflement and interest and to think about translating technical information into personal experience ("Wonder why coal heat feels warmer . . ."). We might say that Beth was responding to her instructor's request that students use their journals to connect course topics with their own experiences. We might also wonder why this entry is as short as it is, and why it jumps from topic to topic as it does. What use could it be for Beth to write so little and to skip from present to past to classroom experience?

Let's next suppose that we also have a transcript of the class meeting before this entry was written, and field notes about ethnographic participant observation before, during, and after class. The transcript might suggest to us that Professor Weber's comment in class that coal heat is "cheaper . . . and dirtier" than other kinds had reminded Beth of her own experience of coal heat (that it feels warmer than other kinds). Weber had asked if anybody had questions about his information on coal heating, but no one had asked any. We might also guess that Beth's conversation, during a break, with two fellow students who asked her how she was preparing for an upcoming class debate prompted her to remark in her journal that "people were getting excited about it."

Finally, let us add the information we could gather from the transcripts of a sequence of open-ended interviews I had with Beth—conversations about why she wrote what she did, how she interpreted her instructor's expectations of journal writing, and what she was doing outside of class. Beth was particularly interested in what her instructor might be expecting, because she felt herself to be deficient as a writer, and she was trying to manage a work schedule that did not give her the time to do what she sensed he wanted his students to do in their journals. To Beth, Professor Weber conveyed a mixed message about his expectations. Although he had described the journal on the assignment sheet as "thinking on paper" and had told students not to worry about grammar and spelling, Beth inferred from another part of the sheet, where entries were called "thoughtful reflections" which students "shall" write five days a week, that her professor—like other teachers who conducted class as he did and rewarded edited and proofread prose—expected academically literate prose of her, writing that was thoughtful, analytical, and free of surface error.

Beth wanted to do well in the course and wanted her journal, which she felt could compensate for poor multiple-choice test performance, to help her realize this goal. She wanted to present herself as an "intelligent thinking college student" to a professor who was her age and shared her love for photography and corny jokes, but who knew vastly more than she about geology, and who, like most of the other male authority figures in her experience, probably could not be trusted to mean everything he said.

Beth told me that when she wrote this entry, she "had in mind what [Professor Weber] said . . . about exponential growth being 'deceptively easy.'" As we talked about this entry, Beth offered an explanation ("it's just what happens when everybody has large families") that showed me she grasped both the principle and the point Weber had made about it in class. But in "slapping down" her journal entry on her way to work, she had deprecated her comprehension both of exponential growth and of the second topic she addressed: coal "facts." Why? She knew this entry "wasn't enough for a full day," but she didn't have or want to take the time to write more, and it frustrated her to expose her unedited and "off the cuff" prose to a literate and expert reader. So she offered a question about coal heat and a comment about the upcoming class debate as a compromise between her interests and her interpretation of Weber's expectations: specifically, in asking the coal question, she compensated for her failure to meet what she understood to be Weber's expectation that journal entries be at least a page or so long by responding to his request in class for questions about his discussion of coal heat and by meeting his expectation that journal keepers connect their own experiences with class topics.

Furthermore, in concluding this entry by expressing enthusiasm for the upcoming class debate, Beth not only served her interest in getting credit for the journal by doing at least something of what her instructor had asked for in it, but also implicitly defined herself in a role vis à vis her fellow students that she became increasingly comfortable expressing in class. This was the role of spokesperson and class leader. Beth asked more questions than other students, and she spoke to the instructor during breaks, trading jokes and anecdotes about their shared hobbies. A transcript of the debate Beth refers to shows that she was one of only two students in the class who took on the roles Weber had asked debaters to enact. He had asked them to debate the pros and cons of nuclear energy development as if they were members of a utility company board, persuading fellow board members either to support development of a nuclear-fired plant or invest in more coal-fired plants. Most students simply explained some part of the issue, reporting information to their classmates. But Beth addressed the group as "Mr. Chairman and members of the board," and she spoke, without a prepared text, to the political concerns such a group would be likely to consider.

In her journal entry, she rehearsed the role of spokesperson for the class—"People already getting excited about tomorrows debate!"—in a way that confirmed her reader's authority as her teacher and as the designer and organizer of this debate activity. Specifically, by expressing enthusiasm for the debate Beth affirmed the enthusiasm Weber had displayed when he said, in class two days earlier, that he wanted "a good, hot, intellectually stimulating debate." Beth was pointing out for him that students were developing the attitude he wanted them to have. Since students' behaviors in class on the day Beth wrote this entry were not likely to have suggested to Weber that they were particularly excited about the debate, Beth also offered her reader a kind of inside information—taken from hall and break conversations—that confirmed his interests as the teacher while it also lent her authority as a spokesperson for the class.

What does this interpretation of Beth's rhetoric in one short journal entry suggest about journal keeping? What does it suggest about how the aims of writing are related to specific, situated social and political facts about human relationships? What are its ramifications for writing-across-the-curriculum programs like the one that encouraged this professor to give this journal assignment? And what does it tell us about research methodology in composition studies, about what our data should be, and how we should find and interpret it? This book explores these questions. As my discussion of Beth's entry shows, the reading of student journals is greatly enhanced when it is supplemented with analysis of transcripts of class meetings and of interviews and conversations with their writers. This is the approach to data I have used in the study reported here.

What follows is an account of journal keeping in an introductory environmental geology course called "Spaceship Earth." Taught in 1986, during the first of two-month-long summer sessions at the University of Northern Iowa, "Spaceship Earth" met five days a week for two hours. The class enrolled 17 students, of various ages and class ranks, and it was taught by an experienced and enthusiastic instructor who was known for his advocacy of writing across the curriculum. This account aims to offer a coherent and systematic interpretation of how this instructor and his students used journal keeping and why they used it as they did. To develop this interpretation, I collected and analyzed the students' journals, transcripts of all class meetings and of multiple interviews with three key informants—two students and the instructor—and various documents pertaining to the conduct of the course and the composition of journal entries. I also attended each meeting of the course as a participant-observer, making notes and collecting impressions.

From these materials emerged an interacting network of relationships: relationships among the histories of individual writers and the rhetoric of their journal texts; relationships among the rhetoric of texts and the agenda and conduct of the "Spaceship Earth" class; and relationships among journal keeping and institutional expectations of the course, its teacher, and its writing assignments. This account centers on connections between journal keeping and class activities; in doing so, it reaches beyond the class itself in two directions: into the experiences and expectations of class participants—students, their teacher, and the researcher—and into the administration of the university, where curricular decisions affecting the course and its writing assignments were made.

Like other ethnographies in literacy and composition, this one describes writing as a sociopolitical process. (See, for example, Doheny-Farina, 1986; Fishman, 1984; Heath, 1983.) But it also has a methodological agenda, which, if implied in other ethnographies, has not been made explicit. I have assumed that the evolution and design of my research activities influenced and were influenced by the people and the writing that I studied I have assumed, that is, that my research activities and the writing activities I studied were interrelated and "reflexive" social processes (Hammersley, 1983). Thus I have tried to account for the conduct of research in the same ways I describe the "product" of my investigation: by showing, that is, how the design of this study—like the writing I interpreted—evolved in a sequence of negotiations.

There are at least three interrelated reasons for the study that generated this account. These reasons involve what we know and don't know about journal keeping, about writing as a socialization process, and about writing as an interdisciplinary learning tool.

Journal Keeping

In American culture and letters, journals have traditionally been associated with self-expression and the personal construction of meaning (North, 1985). The recent popularity of journal keeping as an academic assignment can be traced to Gordon Rohmann's claim, in his 1965 argument against the composition pedagogy of imitation, that journals encourage the "self-actualization" of students, who would learn more by being "honest" in their writing than by imitating the written models of others. Rohmann's claims for the affective uses of journal keeping became a pedagogy in Ken Macrorie's popular 1976 textbook, *Telling Writing.* Five years later, Ira Progoff promoted journal keeping as an explicitly psychotherapeutic tool in his *Journal Workshop* program, which has been adopted for classroom use in college humanities as well as writing courses.

Advocates of journal keeping as a "tool for learning" (Macrorie, 1976) claim that this genre of writing, understood to be "self-sponsored" and "informal," helps students write less apprehensively (Reece, 1981); understand themselves and their ideas better (Fulwiler, 1982); and make better sense, in more "formal" writing assignments, of the academic material they study (Yinger & Clark, 1981). Macrorie has suggested that journal keeping used to generate class discussion can "democratize" the classroom (cited in Fulwiler, 1987). For the most part, proponents of journal keeping substantiate these claims with the testimony of teachers and teacher-researchers and with reference to passages from student-written journal texts.

Formal study of the cognitive uses of what has been called *learner-centered* (Walters & Weiss, 1979) or *expressive* writing has been inconclusive (Harris, 1986). Walters and Weiss assert that "the frequency and amount of learner-centered writing about a subject will increase learning of that subject" and "the concepts that students write about will be clearer to them than the concepts they do not write about," but do not appear to consider the extent to which "learning" in their study was affected by the way "learner-centered" writing assignments were designed, administered, or responded to. Tierney (1981) found that expressive writing helps students remember what they have learned, but Dorsey (1985) found no change in the "syntactic maturity" of students who had kept journals.

Anecdotal accounts of journal keeping in school and college classes conclude that journal writing advances cognition, specifically academic thinking and learning, as well as affective and "personal" growth (Fulwiler, 1982, 1987; Parker & Goodkin, 1987; Selfe & Arbabi, 1986). These accounts tend to cite one or both of two theoretical sources. One is Janet Emig's (1977) argument that writing, unlike other communicative and social behaviors, is an autonomous and essentially cognitive activity. The other is the theory of James Britton, Tony Burgess, Nancy Martin, Alex McLeod, and Harold Rosen (1975), developed in their influential study of two thousand texts written by British schoolchildren, that self-oriented and expressive writing developmentally precedes other-oriented and transactional writing. While implying that the functions of writing are interrelated, Britton uses inferences about writers' relationships with their audiences, derived from inferences about the rhetoric of their texts, to divide functions into three: *expressive writing,* or writing from the self; *transactional writing,* or writing for others; and *poetic writing,* or writing for aesthetic purposes. Britton's theory of the functions of writing has inspired extensive curricular reform and dominated research on journal keeping and other kinds of writing that fall into the expressive category; the journal-keeping assignment which is the focus of this study owes its popularity to the idea that students who use writing to express themselves learn more than they do by producing only the "formal shells" of writing intended to satisfy a reader's requirements (Knoblauch & Brannon, 1983). Citing Emig and Britton, practitioner-researchers such as Toby Fulwiler emphasize the "personal engagement with course materials" prompted by journal keeping (Fulwiler, 1980). Following Peter Elbow, Fulwiler argues that, in order to produce the kind of synthetic and analytic prose expected of them in college, students need the opportunity, first, to spontaneously and personally react in writing to what they have studied.

In associating the function of schoolchildren's texts with the kinds of audiences to which they seemed to be addressed, Britton's work laid a foundation for subsequent study of what makes discourse responsive to particular situations (Herrington, 1985; Odell, 1985). "Adjustment to the audience is inherent in the social contract of all language use," Britton wrote (Britton et al., 1975, pp. 62-63), introducing a discussion of role taking in writing that is borne out in the present study. But analysis of how role taking occurs, or of what, precisely, the rhetoric of audience adaptation has to do with how writing is used or what it is used for, requires a method of study different from Britton's textual analysis. Studies of written texts, in and of themselves, do not tell what their writers intended or how their readers responded; hence, they do not tell how the texts were used.

Britton and his group were aware that expressive writing done in school, for a teacher, does not serve exclusively personal purposes. However, the assumption that journals serve an exclusively self-expressive purpose, wherever and for whomever they are kept, dominates the research and the pedagogy of "writing to learn," of which journal keeping is often a part. Research lags behind pedagogy; since 1982, results of only five formal studies of journal keeping have been made available. All of these assume the expressivity of the documents they analyze. Robinson-Metz (1985) concludes that "journal writing, or a similar type of expressive writing" reveals the "distinctiveness" of individual authors.

A different approach to the functions of journal keeping is exemplified in Roger Shuy's "Dialogue Journal Keeping as a Communicative Event" (Staton, Shuy, & Kreeft, 1982). Shuy uses speech act theory as the basis for his discussion of 15 "language functions" inferred from the texts of sixth graders' journals and their teachers' daily written responses. Shuy argues that form and function in the language of the journals are not isomorphic: when the teacher responds to a repeatedly absent student by "asking" in his journal, "Where have you been on Mondays?" Shuy argues she is really expressing a directive, "Come to school on Mondays." Shuy claims that he "follows a context-based approach using multiple criteria for identifying a particular function" (Staton et al., p. 80). But although the 15 functions that Shuy delineates—"complaining," "questioning," "reporting," and the like—imply what Britton called the "social contract" of language use, they are derived from only one part of what makes that contract: written language. Although Jana Staton introduces this study by saying it "focuses on function and interaction" (p. 12), its methodology directs findings away from a social understanding of function. Because the researchers intended to focus examination on the journal texts "as a phenomenon of value in [their] own right," other writing done in this class or notes of class meetings were not collected. Since relationships between journal keeping and class activities that could reveal writers' relationships to their teacher are not a part of this study, the relevance of writing to the social organization of this class is not examined, and the teacher-informant's intriguing suggestion that "the journals became a central means of mutually negotiating the daily life of the classroom" is not developed. In finding that meaning is "mutually negotiated," Staton et al. raise the question of how real social relationships affect writers' rhetoric. This question has not been addressed in any research on journal keeping to date.

When conclusions about how journals "work" in classes are derived from journal texts alone, journal keeping can appear to be responsible for what supporting information would show to have a variety of sources. (See, for example, Leahy, 1985.) Furthermore, it is not surprising that, for reasons of methodology and ideology, teachers or practitioner-researchers who have informally described the functions of journal keeping tend to find that it helps students mature in intellectual and emotional ways. When journal keeping is studied by teachers who, having assigned their students to keep journals, are predisposed to see the journal as a learning tool (but who don't make examination of their prior interest a part of the research), then, as we might expect, the journal is found to be a learning tool. (See, for example, Hallberg, 1987; Jensen, 1987; Selfe & Arbabi, 1986; Tierney, 1981). Such primarily anecdotal accounts of how journals facilitate learning have generated enthusiastic descriptions of the cognitive and ethical consequences of journal keeping as an academic assignment. But we have seen publication of only one formal study of journal keeping in a university course where writing of this genre might not, typically, be expected (in a course outside an English department, that is—North, 1986a). We know very little about how the rhetoric of journal keeping serves social relationships or about how journal assignments respond to curricular and institutional expectations for writing. To begin to understand what journals are kept for we need to do more than analyze written texts; we need to ask their authors why and for whom they are writing.

The Social and Institutional Contexts of Writing

The world of academic research is reformulating its disciplinary boundaries. We are moving, in the words of Clifford Geertz (1983), toward "repairing" traditional splits between social scientific and humanistic endeavors. Geertz and others have called for studies that combine the interpretation of written texts with the study of the social activities that produce them.

Recent ethnographic research in composition has brought methodologies for the study of social structure to the interpretation of written materials, thereby linking reading, writing, and social behavior.

For her study of writing in two engineering classes, for example, Anne Herrington (1985) collected texts, conducted "discourse-based" and "open-ended" interviews with their authors, interviewed their instructors, and observed, audio-taped, and took field notes. But although Herrington's study describes "social roles and purposes," "social roles" remain rather broadly defined as "student" to "professor" or "expert" to "boss," and the study's focus is on the rhetoric of student writing: that is, how writers' conceptions of their audiences compare with the ways their instructors expect to be addressed. Herrington gives a reading of writing in this class that describes her informants' perceptions of what their writing is for, not an interpretation that sets perceptions and writing in the context of classroom activity. And since she uses frameworks adapted from rhetorical and argumentation theory to analyze written texts, the description of function she arrives at is primarily rhetorical and not social. Like North's (1986a) account of the writing of philosophy students, Herrington's account of writing in chemical engineering classes advances what we know about what writing means to students and teachers, and what they expect of it in courses other than English. But a conception of the writers' "roles" that is adduced from written texts or writers' and readers' comments on them is a rhetorical, and not really a social conception. A social conception of role involves another medium of exchange: talking.

In "The Functions of Writing in an Elementary Classroom," Susan Florio and Christopher Clark (1982) adopt ethnographic methodology to discover the role writing plays in the social and cultural setting of the class. To introduce the class, they use information about the ethnic and socioeconomic backgrounds of students, teacher, and local community. In addition to collecting student writing, they made field notes about and videotapes of the class, they asked the teacher-informant to keep a journal, and they interviewed students about their writing. Discussing the purpose of their study, Florio and Clark "ask . . . in Basso's (1974, p. 432) words 'what position . . . writing occup[ies] in the total communicative economy of the society under study.'" Nonetheless, Florio and Clark choose to identify the purposes of writing as the participants in their study identify them, not as they might be interpreted from the ethnological standpoint Basso's question assumes. Thus, for example, they interpret what to students appeared to be the collaborative development of classroom rules, rules that were actually preselected by their teacher, as "writing to participate in a community." From the sociopolitical perspective on function taken in the present study, this activity would illustrate that student writing is used by the teacher to achieve social control.

That their informants were influenced by the kind of interest Florio and Clark took in them is also not accounted for. With few exceptions (e.g., Odell & Goswami, 1982), ethnographers of composition do not tell their readers how they presented themselves to or how they might have affected their subjects. A document used to illustrate the "writing to occupy free time" function suggests that Florio and Clark made a strong impression on the nine-year-olds they studied: a letter from "Lisa" reads "I love you Susan [Florio]." This letter raises the intriguing, unexplored question of how the children's "writing to occupy free time" reflected the relationships they developed with, in Lisa's words, the "nice, pretty, mature" researchers who spent much of the school day with them.

Although Florio and Clark don't explicate their role in how writing was used in the class they studied, they anticipate a finding of the present study in their demonstration that journal writing—in this case "diary time"—is inhibited when its purposes are ambiguous to students. Children received mixed messages about what diary time was for. Although supposedly private, diaries could be read by the teacher, who kept them with other "official schoolwork," and although students could make their own covers for their diaries, they all had to write on lined school paper Thus Florio and Clark report that it wasn't clear whether diaries had a mainly academic or a mainly social purpose. Given an opportunity to "free write," children wrote notes and cards to each other, but when they were assigned diary time to write, for themselves, about anything they chose, most of them lost interest.

Ann Dyson (1985) demonstrates that the rhetoric of freewriting influences and is influenced by social relationships with others in the classroom in her "Second Graders Sharing Writing." Using observations of children's behaviors as well as their written texts, Dyson describes the kinds of roles three children enacted as they read their freewriting aloud to each other: one seemed to want to entertain the group, another to present herself as a successful and positive person, a third to demonstrate his affiliation with his friends. Dyson's attention to role taking allows her to illustrate that, for the children she studied, writing was "a social process occurring in response to particular situations" (p. 212). But Dyson doesn't attempt to link the dynamics of role playing in writing to the teacher's responses to writing performance or to other class writing activities. And, like most studies of how writing is used in school or college classes, Dyson's does not connect uses of writing to the political structure of the class or the institutional structure of the school.

In general, studies of academic literacy assume, as Scribner and Cole (1981) argue, that the purposes of reading and writing in school are essentially academic: students are taught these "subjects" so that they will be able to use and respond to reading and writing as students should—that is, as their professors do. Thus writing in elementary school is studied as a tool for teaching children how to "do school" (Dyson, 1984), and writing in college is studied as it reflects how students are socialized into disciplinary communities or how they develop as intellectuals (Herrington, 1985; North, 1986a).

Wider ranging accounts of literacy in home, school, and work environments are beginning to interpret writing as a social, cultural, and political process. In studies of writing or literacy in various nonacademic communities, we see writing as it is used in the social and political conduct of daily lives. In the field of composition, perhaps the best known discussion of nonacademic literacy is Shirley Brice Heath's (1983) analysis, in *Ways with Words*, of how children in two Carolina Piedmont communities learn to use language, oral and written, in trying to get what they need from families, schools, and ultimately jobs. The amount of time people in Roadville and Trackton spend writing is little, but it is clear that their doing it is crucial—lists organize shopping, and written forms enable payment of taxes, applications for jobs, and the like. In "Unpackaging Literacy," Sylvia Scribner and Michael Cole's (1981) most accessible discussion of their study of literacy among the Vai people of northern Africa, the authors use the workings of literacy in this culture to argue that academic conceptions of what literacy means (i.e., what it is for) are parochial. What Scribner and Cole identify as journals, for example, have important social, institutional, and political uses in Vai culture. In their journals, the Vai not only record autobiographical events and dreams; they also translate religious texts, and record the names of property deedholders and the outcomes of court cases.

Diary keeping also serves a political purpose in the Old Order Amish schools and homes in southeastern Pennsylvania studied by Andrea Fishman (1984). Several students in the one-room, kindergarten-through-eighth-grade class Fishman observed were "three hour pupils"; they attended school for three hours of the six-hour day, using the other time for vocational training, which typically consisted of helping out with house or farm work. Concerned that outsiders could use the example of three-hour pupils in attacks on the quality of Amish education, the local school board required these pupils to keep diaries recording what they did with their time. These diary entries, Fishman observes, are not used for self-exploration, self-discovery, or autobiographical record; the way they are assigned reflects their political function in the preservation of the school system. Outside the Amish school, journal writing is not popular; Fishman asked children in her informant family to keep journals for her, but none of them wrote more than a page.

How writing can work as an agency for political change is explicitly illustrated in Stephen Doheny-Farina's (1984) *Writing in an Emergent Business Organization: An Ethnographic Study.* Doheny-Farina focuses on how a business plan for a computer software company was written, rewritten, and accepted. His interviews with the authors of this document and observations of their work revealed to Doheny-Farina that discussion of the wording of a particular point in the plan (whether the company should say it would buy a new production facility outright or buy it only under certain productivity conditions) reflected the roles writers wanted to take in controlling the company. The final compromise between the company's president and its board of directors at once expressed and created a restructuring of executive power.

Studies like those of Heath, Doheny-Farina, Fishman, and Scribner and Cole do more than show how writing works as a social and political process. In showing how writing affirms and expresses relationships between people, influences how they think and behave, or develops their authority and power over one another, such studies have also illustrated that various uses of writing necessarily interact. An Amish child's "good night" letter to parents out for the evening, for example, not only helps the child remember and organize what he wants to tell, but also helps affirm an emotional bond; furthermore, as he expresses certain roles in writing this letter, the writing affirms the particular dynamics of his social relationship with his parents. Or, in the software company analyzed by Doheny-Farina, collaboration among authors of the business plan affects their rhetoric in various ways: not only does it lead to changes in the text they produce, but also to subtle changes in the roles they take in relation to each other.

These studies support Marilyn Cooper's (1986) discussion, in "The Ecology of Writing," of how "systems" of texts, ideologies, rhetoric, social relationships, and political hierarchies all interact with one another. Cooper argues that these systems operate dynamically, much the way biological ecologies do. Any text at once responds to and acts on other texts and the people who create them.

Fundamental to this view is the idea that, although discourse may serve personal or private purposes, it functions as a form of social and ultimately political action. In her claim for the public consequences of all discourse, Cooper challenges the view that writers, as "meaning makers" (Berthoff, 1981), deploy their subjective conceptions of audience and subject; Cooper argues that people write to other people as "real social beings." Cooper's examples are not taken from the writing of college students, and she implies that in academia the kind of interaction among texts, ideas, and people that drives the dynamic, ecological model of writing for which she argues may be blocked by role or status differences. But her theory outlines claims that writing is an agency for unlimited and interrelated textual, rhetorical, ideological, social, and political change.

Cooper's theory that writing structures open-ended interaction patterns has yet to be applied or invoked in composition research. But sociologists of education—most of them working in Britain—have produced many illustrations that the political and social relationships of students and teachers affect and are affected by the ideologies brought to the classroom, and the language in which they are expressed (Delamont, 1983; Robinson, 1981; Stubbs, 1983). The theory that guides sociologists to look at the interplay of language, ideas, and social organization is called *symbolic interactionism*. This theory, derived from the social theory of identity developed by George Herbert Mead, holds that people are *reflexive* or self-interacting. From and with other people, they construct the meaning of things interactively, using symbol systems such as language (Delamont, 1983; Robinson, 1981).

For symbolic interactionists, many of whom take an ethnographic approach to the study of language use, the classroom relationship between teacher and student is a joint act, constructed in negotiation. Robinson writes that "acts of teaching both confirm the nature of the social relationship and are permitted by those relationships. . . . Teachers and pupils repeatedly reconstitute that structure, which is both the basis for their interaction and a product of it" (1981, pp. 89-90). Social structure in the classroom reflects political structure; Robinson goes on to say that "ultimately, the teacher is in control; her vocabulary, her orchestration of events underlies that control, and in their role as pupils, children in turn confirm the teacher's authority." For the most part sociologists and sociolinguists who study interaction between teachers and students have used spoken language to infer the social organization of classrooms. They have analyzed how spoken language is used to affirm and construct that organization (Delamont, 1983; Hargreaves, 1972; Stubbs, 1983).

Symbolic interactionists have argued that teachers' power to initiate, manage, and control classroom talk, and hence learning, is constrained not only by their relationships with their students, but also by their social and political relationships with administrators, fellow teachers, and parents. These relationships are, in turn, constrained by teachers' histories—by their histories not only as students and educators, but as people who have learned a particular variety of roles in conducting their lives. Students' responses to teachers, and the kind of power students may exert in a classroom, are likewise influenced by their histories, by their relationships with peers, and by their perceptions of their teachers. Insights like these guided the analysis of journal texts in the present study.

Research in the sociology of education has yet to have much influence on the field of composition, where little work has been done on institutional or political constraints on classroom uses of writing. Perhaps this lack of attention reflects writing teachers' and researchers' political interests in protecting writing as a fundamental tool for the advancement of higher education. The way the discipline of composition defines itself is also a reason for inattention to sociological or political issues. Insofar as composition studies writing, an interdisciplinary and intercultural phenomenon, the field theoretically has fluid boundaries. As an academic discipline, though, the roots of composition are in rhetoric—in writing primarily as an end in itself.

A few studies have addressed institutional or pedagogical constraints on expressive writing, but these are limited to analysis of how teachers' ignorance or failure to communicate effectively with their students prevents writing from being used as the learning tool it ought to be. Healy (1984), for example, finds that a seventh-grade science teacher's interest in using writing in her class was undermined by her lack of knowledge about how to introduce and follow up writing assignments; this conflict affected students' performance in the writing she assigned. Swanson-Owens (1986) finds that high school teachers' values as readers and educators prevented them from following through as expected on plans for using writing in their classes. Research has also considered the influence exerted on student writing by teachers' relationships to their colleagues: Marshall (1984) found that lack of institutional support undermined the effects that expressive writing in high school social science classes might have had.

Largely unexplored, however, in studies of writing across the curriculum or the uses of writing in academia is how writers' rhetoric and the social relationships between writers and readers that are enacted in students' texts are constrained by institutional expectations or by political dynamics in the classroom. One exception is North's (1985) argument that self-sponsored writing in which students and their instructor participate mutually—for example, *dialectic* journal writing like that which Knoblauch and Brannon (1983) call for—is made possible in a classroom where the agenda is negotiated and where power is essentially balanced. Perelman (1986), too, calls for analysis of the "institutional contexts" that constrain the roles of speaker, writer, reader, and audience, pointing out that social roles rehearsed in academic writing assignments are constrained by implicit and explicit institutional rules such as academic freedom (which sanctions forms of personal and unevaluated writing), and, perhaps more powerfully, the rule that teachers evaluate students.

Recent discussion and ethnographic study of the contexts of writing in academia are painting a dynamic and interactive picture of the relationships between writers and readers, students and teachers, classes and institutions. Brandt (1986), Cooper (1986), North (1985), and Perelman (1986) are among those who have suggested the need for study of how college writers and readers (and researchers studying them) affect and are affected by each other's responses. But research into writing as a social or political process has focused on elementary classrooms or "real-world" communities. Perhaps we have not looked at college classes as social communities because, as David Bartholomae (1985) has argued, we overlook the extent to which academic success is the outcome of a socializing process.

On the other hand, North, Perelman, and others have suggested that students' writing reflects the political dynamics of class-rooms: that the roles enacted by writer and reader are con-strained by the locus of authority and power in the classroom and institution. If, theoretically, writing has unlimited potential to change what people think and do, when we look at our univer-sities as social and political institutions we begin to see how writing works to shape the interests of those who manage them.

The Uses of Writing Across the Curriculum

Interest in various contexts for learning—social and institu-tional as well as cognitive and ethical—is reflected in a popular curricular reform movement advocating writing across the cur-riculum. Although writing-across-the-curriculum programs all hold to the premise that writing should be learned and used in "context," which context or contexts it should be learned and used in—and what it should be used for—has been debated. Those who say that writing should be taught and used to help students master the rhetoric of academic, disciplinary, or professional communities (for example, Faigley & Hansen, 1985; Herrington, 1985; Jolliffe, 1984) challenge those who have called for writing assignments that help students develop intellectually and ethi-cally in a more general sense. (See the essays in Fulwiler, 1987, and in Young & Fulwiler, 1986.)

The latter, "expressivist" group (so named in Faigley, 1986) has been fueled by rhetorical theory that predates the current move toward academic or disciplinary contextualism. Drawing on Britton et al.'s (1975) observation that, developmentally, self-expressive writing precedes transactional writing, expressivists like Peter Elbow (1981) maintain that writing for self-expression or discovery—free from the constraints of audience—is profitable preparation for writing for an audience. It allows the writer to think through ideas, try on new voices, and develop fluency. Journal keeping, freewriting, and other informal writing as-signments are geared toward freeing the writer's inner self and aiding in the discovery of what one really thinks or means or knows. Expressive writing, it is thought, frees the writer to articulate emotions and encourages the exploration of personal experience; connecting abstract concepts to concrete personal experience improves the writer's understanding of those concepts. Writing is a mode of learning (Emig, 1977). And writing, especially the fluent, unencumbered kind encouraged in journals, hones thinking skills as well. Fulwiler (1986, p. 25) claims that writing "is the specific activity which most promotes independent thought," and that expressive writing does this most effectively. For most expressivists, it is irrelevant whether writing is done in a journal, as an essay, or as notes, as long as the writer explores ideas with sincerity and in depth. "Context" is less important than the inner life and cognitive abilities of the writer.

The ideology of the expressivists remains powerful, in part because it implies a pedagogy for "writing to learn" across the curriculum that has been relatively easy to implement. Training workshops for faculty from various disciplines often stress the value of writing as a way for students to think through problems or come to grips with course material in a more personal way than simply by learning "facts." Since this sort of writing does not have to be graded, often being considered too personal for evaluation, faculty pressed for time find it attractive. Journal keeping is particularly well-suited to writing across the curriculum, and to general education courses, because, according to Fulwiler, journals are "interdisciplinary and developmental by nature" (1982, p. 30). However, although expressive writing practices have seemed easily adaptable to courses across the curriculum, the results of their use have been hard to evaluate.

Social process approaches to composition, on the other hand, imply that what students learn from writing is not simply a function of what kinds of writing they do (or the kinds of writers they are), but also a function of the social and political structure of particular classes, disciplines, and institutions—in other words, the context. As Brodkey, a social process theorist, puts it, "writing is a social practice" (1987, p. i). Rather than view writing as a means to enhance abstract cognitive skills, social process theorists call for writing in various contexts that will initiate students into unique disciplinary or professional rhetorics, a task that they often see best accomplished by means of analysis of professional models and composition of documents like those found in the discipline under study. They value transactional over expressive writing, stressing that transactional writing that contributes to the construction of knowledge within a discipline is just as educationally challenging and indicative of intellectual growth as is writing that expresses one's feelings or explores personal experience. Jolliffe (1984) argues, furthermore, that assigning expressive writing as a means of discovery in a discipline-specific class will do little to teach students how practitioners of that discipline write. From the perspective of the social process school, writing-across-the-curriculum classes that fail to show students how practitioners write do not fulfill their mission. Based on the rationale that writing is a sort of conversation between texts within a discipline, other pedagogical techniques advocated by social process theorists emphasize the value of social interaction, of talk, peer critiques, or peer tutoring, for example (Bruffee, 1978, 1984). While expressivists use some collaborative techniques as well, they see collaboration as sharing ideas; in contrast, social process advocates talk about constructing knowledge as a group.

The task the social process theorists have generally set for themselves is to discover the specific rhetoric of each academic discipline (Bazerman, 1983). But disciplinary boundaries are fuzzy, making this task quite difficult. And in school, writing instruction is also inevitably affected by the sociopolitical role that writing plays in the classroom and in the university, in structuring authority between students and teachers, novices to the discipline and experts in it (Bartholomae, 1985; Bizzell, 1982). As we change the part that writing plays in university curricula, we alter roles and relationships in which teachers, students, and administrators are deeply entrenched. This issue has been addressed (e.g., Perelman, 1986), but not in research into how writing is used and what it is used for in university classes.

Writing across the curriculum has received a great deal of publicity; programs have been shaped by a growing literature advocating various policies and strategies. But for all we know about what journals, freewriting, and other expressive techniques can or should do, we know very little about how they actually work in classes throughout the academic disciplines. When we challenge the distinction between expressive and transactional writing that has governed research on journal keeping, and when we assume, instead, that the rhetoric of privately produced writing— no less than the rhetoric of other kinds of writing—represents social, cultural, and institutional awareness, then we can begin to address questions about how students and teachers use this awareness to negotiate their meanings and intentions in journal assignments.

As I see it, my account of what writing was used for in "Spaceship Earth" is an interpretation of how writing shaped and was shaped by the social and institutional structure of the community in and for which it was written. In a classroom, social structure is comprised of relationships among class participants, typically students and teacher. These relationships can be adduced from the kinds of roles participants take in relation to each other, roles that are expressed in the ways they understand and communicate with each other (Hargreaves, 1972). I will suggest that the journal entries express their authors' perceptions of the kinds of roles to take in relation to their reader, roles that were shaped by their histories, by their expectations, and by the way they communicated with their reader during and in connection with this class.

The materials I collected shaped my interpretation of how journal keeping worked in "Spaceship Earth." Had I analyzed only the texts of journals kept for this class, I might have found evidence for the claims Britton and others have made for the nature and function of expressive writing. But reading the journals in light of what happened in class—what was talked about, how it was talked about, and who talked—told a rather different story.

Students were assigned to make connections in their journals among their own experiences of geological processes and hazards, their reading of current events in geology, and, as their instructor put it, the "rather abstract" material presented in lectures and the textbook. However, like Beth, many students used most of their entries not to "reflect," as directed, on connections among their experiences in and outside of class. Instead they carried on a one-sided conversation with the instructor (who didn't read their entries until the course was over). In this conversation, they commented, for the most part, on class or class-related activities. Many used their journals to help prepare for tests and for the one class activity in which they were required to participate actively. When we ask what caused this apparent discrepancy between students' uses for their journals and their instructor's intentions, we are drawn into considering the way the class was conducted, the way the assignment was designed, and the particular interests and expectations of individual writers.

Journal keeping appeared to play a limited part in the class. Rarely was it referred to or used. Yet when we consider who talked when, what was talked about, and how the agenda was established, we find that, indirectly, the journal assignment had a great deal to do with the way the class was conducted. Rather like a subplot, it was crucial to the development of the main plot, which, from a social and functional perspective, was the development of the teacher's performance for his students, and theirs for him.

Given the instructor's advocacy of writing across the curriculum, and his ambitious goals for journal keeping, why wasn't the "Spaceship Earth" journal assignment designed and handled so as to play a larger and more explicit part in the conduct of the class? Why wasn't journal keeping used as a vehicle for communication or as a way of decentralizing authority, as it might have been if entries had been shared, read, or discussed? The answer can be found by examining the instructor's background and expectations and his goals as a (nontenured) faculty member, students' expectations of their instructor's performance, and institutional expectations of the course. All interacted to shape the role journal keeping played in class dynamics.

Mine is but one of many possible answers to the question of how writing functioned in this class. With the material I collected, other viable readings of its uses could be constructed, readings that, for example, might take a psychoanalytic, feminist, or Marxist approach to the uses of writing in this setting. My primary concern is that the view I have taken here be coherent, persuasive, and responsible to my data. Someone else looking at the material I interpreted should be able to see how and why I arrived at the interlocking network of personal, social, and institutional uses for writing that is depicted here.

2

PROCEDURES: REFLEXIVITY IN CLASSROOM COMPOSITION RESEARCH

Like the ethnographies of writing or literacy described in the preceding chapter, this study of the functions of journal keeping in a university science class interprets what writing tells about the social community in which I assumed it to be embedded. As I will show in this chapter, I designed the study so that my interpretation of writing would be derived from the particulars of the social setting in which I examined it, a university science class. I did not intend, finally, to test conceptual frameworks that were derived from studies of writing in other settings (Goetz & LeCompte, 1984); rather, I used information gathered from class participants to develop an account of how journal keeping worked to express and affirm the social dynamics of this community.

The procedures I used to gather and interpret information are fairly standard practice in the conduct of ethnographic research. In order to locate the function of journal texts not only in the texts themselves, but in the interactions of writers and readers in the science class, I audited class meetings and recorded students' and teacher's behaviors, as did Florio and Clark, Dyson, and Herrington; I interviewed and closely followed the progress of volunteer informants, as did Heath and Fishman; and, like all the ethnographic researchers whose work I've cited, I paid close attention to the attitudes, behaviors, and ideas of the people whose writing I collected and analyzed.

Nonetheless, my account of the design and conduct of this study is informed by a methodological assumption that theorists of ethnography have articulated (e.g., Hammersley, 1983; North, 1987) but that practitioners of ethnography in composition have not invoked. Called the *principle of reflexivity* by sociologist of education Martin Hammersley, this implies that the activities of research are no less a social enterprise than is the subject of study. Because the research process of an ethnographic study like this one directs the interpretation that is its outcome, my research actions, in Hammersley's words, are "open to analysis *in the same terms* as those of other participants."

To explain why the evolution of this study is as much its subject as is my analysis of students' texts, I will first discuss my methodological assumptions, describing what reflexivity implies for the conduct of this ethnography and how the term *role* will be used to characterize the social interactions in which my research evolved. Then I will describe the phases of this research, showing how they were social and reflexive activities.

Methodological Background: Reflexivity in Ethnography

My understanding that what I studied and how I studied it are social enterprises originates, philosophically, in the ontological premise that the world of humane experience is social and cultural; the meaning of an activity or phenomenon resides in the way it serves the interaction of people, regulating that interaction or expressing its regulation. Thus I assume, as Marilyn Cooper (1986) has argued, that any writing, no matter how personal or private, reveals social experience or makes social history. Some texts (journal entries, for example) may not explicitly be written to inform, persuade, or please a reader, but because the author of any text necessarily learned to write in response to someone else's direction, all writing is forged in social awareness.

Working from this assumption, ethnographers study writing as it naturally occurs in a particular social setting, observing and "inscribing" that setting in field notes, and then interpreting what writing means, either to particular people in that setting (Dyson, Florio & Clark), or to their social community (Doheny-Farina, 1986; Fishman, 1984; Heath, 1983; Scribner & Cole, 1981). My work falls in the latter category: because I assume that the function of writing is the part it plays in social structure, I used my interpretation of the journal keeping of individual writers and readers in this class to develop a picture of how this writing served the interactions among them.

Studying an activity as it naturally occurs in a social situation is traditionally known as *participant observation* (Long, 1980). For purposes of analytical clarity, Goetz and LeCompte (1984) and Long (1980) describe participant observer ethnography as if the observer and participant roles were independent of each other. However, all activity is social, and no ethnographer simply observes; she also, simultaneously, participates. My view is that all people occupying a particular setting are linked in what Cooper (borrowing Vygotsky's term) compares to a "web" of social expectations. Thus, the investigator's presence inevitably affects the community under study, while it also affects her understanding of that community. Not only did my presence affect the people whose work I studied, but those people meanwhile affected the way I studied their work and, thus, the conclusions I drew from it.

The principle of reflexivity applies this idea, not only to the community under study, but to the activity of studying the community as well. In opening my actions to the same kind of analysis I will apply to other participants in this research, I will show that, just as my informants' histories and expectations—as, for example, students, teacher, and journal keepers—shaped the roles they expressed in their writing, so my own history as a journal keeper and my expectations of this research predisposed me to take certain roles in interacting with others involved in the project. Furthermore, like the choices my informants made in their writing, my procedural and interpretive choices represent compromises: decisions that others' interests constrained. These interests included the expectations and needs of my informants and of readers and evaluators of this study.

Reflexivity, then, names my assumption that my informants' interests interacted with mine to shape the conduct of this study and the interpretation of writing that evolved in it. In showing how that interaction took place, I use the term *role* to name positions people took in relation to each other. Like sociologists of education David Hargreaves and Sara Delamont, I define role as a particular position with which characteristic expectations are associated. These expectations are often shaped or defined by those of a complementary position. Because, for example, a person taking the role of *teacher* is most likely to do so in response to other(s) taking the complementary roles of students, *teacher* can be defined as the position for a person who responds in a certain way to other people in the role positions of *student*. When my teacher informant responded to me by answering my questions about his teaching experience, he took the role of *interview subject* in response to my role of *interviewer*. However, when he asked for my opinion, then what he expected of me—his role in relation to me—shifted, changing my expectations and role in relation to him. This shift affected the way we subsequently responded to each other, the kind of information he gave me, and the way I interpreted that information.

Thus reflexivity implies for my account of this study not only that it took place in a sequence of social interactions, but also that it *evolved* as my and others' expectations and roles shifted. I began the research with a topic that, as I will show, personal and professional interests inclined me to pursue. As I was finding a topic and setting in which to study it, I was also identifying problems that were later focused by the way I collected data and recorded it. Meanwhile, the way I presented myself and my research to informants affected their responses to me, the writing they chose to share with me, and the way I would interpret that writing. Thus the research procedures described in this chapter—finding a topic, identifying problems, finding and entering a setting, collecting and inscribing data, and developing an interpretation—name overlapping and interconnected activities.

Finding a Topic

As North (1987) points out, ethnographies in composition have mostly differed from ethnographies in anthropology or sociology in that they interpret writing (or reading) in the context of a social community, without intending to address the more comprehensive topic of what structures that community. As it turned out, I ended this research project by analyzing how writing served social and political relationships; but when I began it, by virtue of my professional affiliation, I was more interested in studying a particular kind of writing than a particular community, or kind of community. Although my interpretation of journals was directed by the particulars of the social setting for which they were written, my role as a researcher of writing predisposed me to look at writing—and not, for example, talk or nonverbal behavior—as an agency for social structure.

Much as my professional bias as a researcher inclined me to use writing to show what other activities in a classroom community might reveal just as well, my personal experience as a journal keeper and writing teacher/tutor also inclined me to see as relevant to communication a genre of writing—journal keeping—that, as my review of the literature suggests, scholars in composition have typically linked to self-expression. I kept a journal, sporadically, throughout my high school and college years, but I was not likely to do so when I could communicate directly with whomever the writing was about or for. In connection with teaching or tutoring writing, I have often advised journal keeping, but this advice has resulted in sustained production of journal entries only when these entries have been used to develop communication between writer and reader. For example, when a tutee, at my suggestion, brought journal entries about memories of her childhood to our meetings, I was moved to respond in kind, and with our shared entries, our friendship developed. Although I was not consciously aware of a connection when I began this study, this experience surely planted a seed for research that grew to focus on the communicative function of journal keeping. In addition, the uses made of journal keeping in classes at the university where I worked affected the kinds of problems I would identify, and my professional roles at this university affected my approach to studying them. As consultant to faculty and to students in matters related to writing, I was in a position to see writing assignments from two points of view. Discrepancies between faculty and student perceptions and responses to journal keeping led me to identify the problems I describe below.

Identifying Problems

When I was ready to begin this research in 1986, there were many opportunities to study journal keeping as a class assignment at the University of Northern Iowa. In my role as consultant to faculty interested in using or improving writing in their classes, I was in a good position to see how instructors chose to assign and use journals. Meanwhile, as director of a writing tutoring program, I was also in a position to cross-check faculty descriptions of assignments with their students' descriptions and with printed assignment directions. I found some discrepancy between teachers' conceptions of a journal and their students' conceptions. Like North (1986b), I found that the journal was not one, but many assignments. Students' and instructors' expectations, descriptions, and the roles they took as journal readers or writers varied across and within disciplines.

It seemed to me that journal keeping could be a flexible tool, a laboratory opportunity for writing to serve the goals of particular courses. But some UNI faculty seemed to be giving their students mixed messages about the purposes and audiences for journal entries. For example, in a literature course, journals were assigned as an occasion for spontaneous and "gut reaction" writing, but the entries were evaluated by a reader whose comments suggested she expected edited prose. In a physics class where the journal was described as a written dialogue, the reader's part in the "conversation" consisted of brief, encouraging remarks. Students in an introductory theater class were told to "write for [them]selves," but each entry was to follow a specified format. With this and other anecdotal evidence, I wrote a paper arguing that instructors needed to review the goals of their courses and their expectations of journal entries before deciding how and for what purposes to assign journals.

A colleague's (angry) reaction to this paper prompted me to rephrase my conclusion as a broad question for a more extensive investigation of the pedagogy of journal keeping: How was this assignment being made? Preliminary review of the literature on expressive writing led me to pose two related questions, one about the rhetoric of journal keeping, the other about journal keeping and cognition. First, in what sense could students write for themselves in work to be turned in to teachers? My notes about possible research methods in the spring of 1986 show that I thought composing protocols aloud as well as text analyses and discourse-based interviews of the sort Odell and Goswami (1982) and Herrington (1985) conducted would give me insight into this problem. Second was the problem of how journal writing was related to learning. Here was a very broad question: How was I going to define *learning*?

As I have suggested, I was personally interested in what makes journal writing seem to work, professionally concerned that this assignment was causing frustration for students and faculty, and philosophically predisposed to take an ethnographic approach to studying this problem. Furthermore, my professional roles made this kind of approach feasible: in order to carry out my responsibility to consult with faculty on writing assignments, I needed the detailed, situation-specific information about assignment design and outcomes that ethnographic classroom research provides. Thus the answers to the questions I had posed—how is a journal assignment made, who are entries written for, and what is learned in writing them—would depend on whose assignment I chose to study and what class I chose to study it in.

Finding a Setting

I was ready, in March 1986, to look for that class. To learn how the journal assignment was designed and presented, I needed to be able to collect relevant written descriptions and to hear how the instructor described this assignment to me and to the class. To find out who student journal keepers understood to be the audience for their entries, and what they learned from them, I needed to be able to read journal entries and interview their authors. To find out how writers' perceptions of their purpose and audience might change or develop during the period of the course, I needed to be able to collect writing and discuss it with its authors at frequent and regular intervals. Having decided that I wanted to learn what writing meant to students and teacher and how it served the social community of their class, I needed (like Florio and Clark or Dyson) to be able to audit the class and discuss its dynamics with the student informants whose texts I read and with the teacher who read them.

Thus my choice of a setting would be directed by my finding a faculty informant who not only assigned journals in a class I could feasibly study, but who also was willing to give me extensive access to written materials generated in and for this class, expose his or her teaching to my observation, and describe for my record his or her history and experience as a writer, educator, and teacher of this class. As I've indicated in describing how reflexivity applies to the conduct of this study, my prospective informant's needs and expectations would affect my choice of a research site, the way I entered it and behaved in that setting, and ultimately what I took from it. In the following description of how "Spaceship Earth" came to be the setting for this study, I will show why I was inclined to ask its instructor for his cooperation and why he was inclined to cooperate with me.

I met my faculty informant at the University of Northern Iowa Writing Across the Curriculum workshop in 1983, where I learned that he assigned students to keep journals in his introductory environmental geology course called "Spaceship Earth." A 43-year-old assistant professor in the earth science department, with a career in government and industry behind him, Carl Weber was an experienced teacher and writer. Actively interested in giving students more opportunities to practice writing in his and other general education courses, Weber, in the fall of 1984, asked a colleague and me what he could do to have students in "Spaceship Earth" write critical reviews that were more like what he expected to read. At our suggestion, Weber made model reviews available to his students and, with our help, he organized the several hundred students enrolled in the multisection class into small peer critique groups. Then, in the summer of 1984, in response to Weber's concern that his tests in "Spaceship Earth" might be "too hard," my colleague audited a few class meetings, setting a precedent for me to audit the class two years later.

In the spring of 1985, before I had made any plans to study journal keeping, I invited Weber to speak to our tutoring staff about his writing assignments; he impressed us with his interest in the process of expressing and revising ideas in writing. Weber described his journal assignment and the peer critique activities. He left a document with us that he also made available to his own students called "The Evolution of a Paper"; this was a series of drafts, with Weber's comments, of an article that he ultimately published.

Weber's interest in writing, his enthusiasm and popularity as a teacher, and the good working relationship I had developed with him thus predisposed me in 1986 to consider "Spaceship Earth" the most suitable of several courses I might use as a setting for studying journal keeping. The timing of this course was convenient; unlike other courses I considered, it was offered in the summer of 1986, when I wanted to begin the research. Furthermore, the cosmological and environmental topics addressed in Weber's course—from the earth's origin in the Big Bang to its potential demise in nuclear winter—interested me more than did the subjects of alternative research prospects ("Foreign Language Teaching" or a general education philosophy/religion course, "The Human Person").

I pursued my interest in observing and studying journal keeping in "Spaceship Earth," not only for these reasons, but also because Weber, for his own professional and political reasons, wanted me to do so. First, I learned later that Weber thought he might need testimony about his teaching ability, which a tenure and promotion review committee had challenged. Given our mutually satisfactory working relationship, Weber was likely to have expected that my observing his class would give him incentive to use his teaching skills to their best advantage, and, in turn, lead me to support his teaching.

Second, my interest in studying a summer session of "Spaceship Earth" was useful for Weber because he was freer in the summertime to "experiment," as he put it, with his syllabus and his teaching methods. He preferred to try out new methods during the summer session, because the review committee visited classes and student evaluations were expected only in the fall and spring semesters. Thus, were I to audit his summer 1986 "Spaceship Earth" class, he would be in a position to demonstrate untried methods for an interested observer, without jeopardizing—and perhaps improving—his position with the tenure review committee. Although it turned out that Weber decided not to experiment with the summer environmental geology course, I think we both understood that my observing the class would be mutually advantageous. In choosing to do so, I narrowed the focus of my investigation: because the four-week summer section of "Spaceship Earth" would have fewer students and a more compressed schedule than the fall and spring sections, I would study writing in the context of a particular class, and my findings might not apply to other sections of the course or to the larger disciplinary community of geology courses at UNI.

Two months elapsed between the time Professor Weber agreed to cooperate with me in a study of his class and the day I introduced my project to his class. During that period, from March to June of 1986, Weber and I negotiated the way I would enter and respond to the setting of "Spaceship Earth." My position was influenced by the interests of my dissertation advisor, the UNI Graduate College Research Office (from whom I needed approval for my human subject research plans), and my superior in the Office of Learning and Instruction (from whom I needed permission to take time off). Although it could be useful for me to discuss the involvement of all these people in my research plans, Professor Weber's interest in these plans was the most relevant to the conduct of the course when I studied it. In the next section, I will show how my plans to enter the setting of "Spaceship Earth" evolved in my negotiations with Weber.

Entering the Setting

Negotiating My Role in "Spaceship Earth"   In late March 1986, assuming that Weber was planning to assign his summer session

"Spaceship Earth" students to keep journals, I asked him if I could use his class as a setting for a study of journal keeping. Weber said he hadn't assigned journals since the previous summer; he had dropped the assignment in response to his promotion review committee's assessment that his student evaluations—containing a number of unfavorable responses to writing assignments—needed, he said, to be "brought up." But because he liked this assignment, which would not be subject to evaluation in the summer session, he said he had "thought about" restoring it. Weber told me later that summer that he would "probably" have decided to restore the assignment whether or not I had wanted to study it, but given his interest in my supporting his teaching, it seems likely that my interest in using his class as a research site influenced his decision.

In mid-April of 1986, Weber invited me to use his class for research, and I sent him a written description, reproduced as Figure 1, of my understanding of the "Research Purpose," "Questions," "Procedural [matters]," "Participant selection," and my "Reservations." Weber was satisfied with this proposal, and on April 24, in the role of a researcher interviewing an informant, I met with him to gather information about the history of "Spaceship Earth" and his writing assignments for the course. I intended to influence Weber's plans for the course as little as possible, yet in order to sustain in our relationship the particular blend of mutual respect and collegial familiarity that encouraged Weber to confide in me, I needed at this point to be willing to take an interested and advisory role in the design of his class.

My sense that a shift in my role was being called for was prompted by a shift in Weber's role: Weber responded to me for most of the meeting as an interview *subject* (he did not, that is, ask for my opinions, comments, or advice), but as our meeting came to a close, when I asked for information about the journal assignment, he responded to me as an *interviewer*: that is, he asked my opinion. Specifically, Weber appeared to interpret a question that I asked to gain information as a question with a hidden advisory agenda. When I asked, "Would you respond to the journals—I mean, read them and give them back with comments—if you had time during the semester?" Weber responded, "I haven't been doing that—as I said, I think I should stay out of the journals—but it might be a good idea if I had the time. I take it you think it's a good idea." Later in the conversation, after I had turned off the tape-recorder, Weber asked, "Would you suggest having [students] share [read and respond to] each other's journals?"

Despite Weber's interest in my advice, I tried at first to protect my new role as observer. My notes of this conversation show that although I thought the journal keeping in his class would be better received if students had a reader for their entries, I was reluctant to offer my opinion because, "having presented myself to [Weber] as a researcher now, I don't feel comfortable starting to tell him what he should be doing with the journal." My resistance to shifting roles in relation to Weber was prompted by resistance to the possibility of changing my expectations of the research: I was not then planning to study journals that were responded to or were part of a dialogue. I did not yet grasp how communication with others is relevant to what it means to "write for the self" in an academic context.

However, my interest in sustaining my informant's confidence by offering him advice proved to be stronger, at this point, than my interest, as a researcher, in the rhetoric of journal keeping and my corresponding role as an outsider to the design of this class. My experience as a writing tutor, and my reading of student journals that Weber left with me, prompted me to write Weber a few days later that "there are some good reasons to make . . . the journal a part of a dialogue, with you or with peers in the class."

Shortly after I offered this opinion, however, Weber and I resumed the roles of informant and researcher. As I will show in Chapter 5, Weber's history as a writer and teacher, and his expectations and objectives for "Spaceship Earth," inclined him not to "interfere," as he put it, by responding to the journal entries. On the other hand, as an advocate of teaching methods which made use of writing, and as a colleague who had expressed interest in my advice, he was also not inclined to reject it completely. He told me there was too much material for him to cover in the four-week summer course—which met Monday through Friday for two hours each day—to allow time for students to read each other's journals or for him to respond to them while the class was in session. However, in a move to satisfy what he perceived to be my expectations, Weber offered to give me his responses to the journals after the course ended.

In the research plan I had given Weber in mid-April, I had said I would audit the class meetings when the journal assignment was made and when journals were used in class. But on June 6, when I met with Weber to show him the flyer I planned to give his students, his interest in my "following" his teaching, as he put it,

FIGURE 1
_____

MY RESEARCH PLANS FOR PROFESSOR WEBER, APRIL 1986

To follow up on our phone conversation the other day, here is
my thinking about how a journal assignment in your Spaceship
Earth class could provide information for a study of journal
keeping in academia.

Research Purpose:

Various studies have reported generally on how journals
promote learning in writing across the curriculum efforts, but,
to my knowledge, we have no detailed account of the process and
outcomes of journal keeping from both students' and instructors'
perspectives. I have also begun to see that the journal
assignment throughout the disciplines varies radically in its
purpose, audience, and relationship to other writing assignments
and to course goals. I believe this variance needs to be
documented in some detail if we are to understand the
relationship between journal keeping and "learning." Preliminary
observations of journal keeping, interviews with journal writers
and readers and analyses of entries should help focus the
purposes of this research.

Questions:

What are the goals/purposes of the course in question?

Why has the instructor chosen to make this assignment?

How does the instructor describe the assignment?

How is the assignment made?

How does the student describe the assignment?

How does the student describe the purpose of the assignment?

How does the student describe the audience for the assignment?

How, according to instructor and students, is the journal
keeping related to other assignments?

How is it related to the goals of the course?

How does the student describe the process of making journal
entries?

How are the entries related?

FIGURE 1 (CONT.)

_____

MY RESEARCH PLANS FOR PROFESSOR WEBER, APRIL 1986

How do the entries compare with other writing for the course?

How are the entries responded to?

etc.

Procedural:

Interview instructor before course begins.

Audit class when journal assignment is made; collect all materials about the course that are distributed to students.

Identify participants for study; interview.

Teach participants to compose on audiotape; collect compose aloud for several entries.

Collect all of participants' writing generated in relation to this class.

Analyze journal entries, notes and materials submitted for evaluation; identify cues to audience awareness and purpose.

Participant selection:

Student and instructor participation should be voluntary. Because detailed information will be more important to me than a general survey, I foresee working with closely 3 or 4 students in each class. It should be emphasized that my role is simply to collect information, not to offer suggestions or guidance. I may offer a modest financial incentive to participants. Participants should, above all, be comfortable with writing and with talking about their writing. They will perhaps have had some experience keeping a personal or academic journal. They should be willing to compose journal entries on audiotape and they should be able to make available about an hour a week for conversation with me about the journal keeping.

Reservations:

The process and outcomes of journal keeping in a 4 week class may and probably will be unlike those of a 15 week semester class.

prompted me to consider what I could gain from auditing as many meetings as possible. I wanted to know, as my research proposal for Weber had read, "how journal keeping is related to the goals of the course." To see how Weber put those goals in writing for his students, I needed only to look at his syllabus; but to see in its daily routines what purposes this class served for its participants, I needed to audit as many meetings as possible.

Thus my plans to study how the journal was assigned and responded to in "Spaceship Earth" evolved in a process of give and take with my key informant. Although my advisory role in relation to Weber's conduct of the summer course ended after our April meeting, the history of our professional relationship would subtly but inevitably affect my role as researcher and "student" of his class. For example, Weber introduced me to his class as a "Writing Specialist" (my title) who planned to do research with the "Spaceship Earth" journals. I was presented to the class, not simply as a naive outsider, but as a professional with a speciality in writing.

Despite this introduction, I tried to enter this setting unobtrusively, so as to be able to understand it as a participant would (Goetz & LeCompte, 1984). As an ethnographer, I wanted to minimize my effect on the interaction among students and between students and professor in this class. Nonetheless, much as my research plans and the roles I took in articulating them affected my faculty informant's plans for writing in his class, so my expectations and the roles I took in articulating them as I introduced the project on the first day of class likewise affected my student informants. My entrance into the setting of the class set the stage for the sequence of negotiations that would characterize my interaction with student informants and influence my interpretation of their journal writing.

Introducing the Research Project to Students "Spaceship Earth" was conducted in a spacious but windowless amphitheater style lecture hall in a three-story, ten-year-old building of science laboratories and classrooms. On the first day of class, I sat near the front of the hall, at the end of the row of seats closest to the bank of cabinets which served as Weber's podium. For a logistical reason—I wanted to be sure Weber's introduction to the course would be audibly recorded—I chose this vantage point to introduce my project to the class and to invite the cooperation of a manageable number—four or five—student informants.

Before introducing me to the class, Weber described the journal assignment and showed some overhead projections of sample entries. One of these referred to its author's enjoyment at the "Professor standing high in the air playing with [a] slinky." As I stood up to introduce my research project, my joking reference to this comment ("Do we have to pay extra for the demonstrations, Carl?") may have served to show the class that I was comfortable —and on equal footing—with their instructor, to whom I referred by first name, and that I would act on his earlier comment that this would be an "informal" class. The function of my opening remark, then (using term *function* as I will use it in describing my informants' work), was to encourage the informality that Weber (and I, too) wanted to establish.

After distributing a handout (Figure 2) that anticipated my oral presentation, I went on to introduce my project, describing its rationale, explaining what I wanted all the students to do, and suggesting what participation could do for students who agreed to be my informants. I first asked the group of 17 students how many had kept journals, logs, or reading diaries in connection with any school work or classes they had taken; the number of hands raised (eight) gave me reason to say that journal keeping of one kind or another was evidently a popular writing assignment, and that we needed to know more about what keeping a journal in school involves.

Then I described the purposes of my study and what participation would require. I asked for (and received) permission from all 17 students to read and copy their journals when they were handed in at the end of the term, and to observe and take notes during class. In addition, I asked for volunteers to serve as my informants, describing what this would entail. First, informants needed to be willing to let me duplicate, twice a week, all the writing they had done in connection with this class: not only journal entries, but notes taken in class, tests, and drafts of any (extra credit) formal papers, too. Second, they needed to be willing to meet with me, twice a week, to discuss the writing I had collected from them and their reactions to the course. My description of what informants' participation in the research would entail presumably attracted students confident enough of their writing to be willing to share it with a stranger, and interested enough in the course to be willing to take the time to talk about it. I explained that all participants' identities would remain confidential, and that cooperation with me would not affect grading; nonetheless, the incentives I offered to prospective informants

FIGURE 2

DESCRIPTION OF RESEARCH PROJECT DISTRIBUTED TO SPACESHIP EARTH STUDENTS,

 University of Northern Iowa

OFFICE OF LEARNING AND INSTRUCTION
BARTLETT EAST

Cedar Falls, Iowa 50614
273-2346

June 9, 1986

TO: Students in SPACESHIP EARTH, June 1986

FROM: ANNE JOHNSTONE, Writing Specialist
      237 Bartlett   Phone # 273-3489

YOU ARE INVITED TO PARTICIPATE IN A STUDY OF THE JOURNAL ASSIGNMENT

WHAT IS THE PURPOSE OF THIS STUDY?

    Its essential purposes are to find out what keeping a journal for this class involves, to find out what participants learn or don't learn from keeping a journal, and to see how journal keeping is related to other aspects of this course.

WHAT WILL PARTICIPATION ENTAIL?

  --<u>Willingness to have all writing you do for this class duplicated, at no cost to you, for the purposes of this research.</u> Writing includes class notes, quizzes and exams, drafts and final copy of term paper, and journal entries. ALL MATERIALS SUBMITTED FOR THIS STUDY REMAIN CONFIDENTIAL. Identities of participants will not be disclosed in any publication related to this study.

  --<u>Willingness to discuss your work for this class in regular meetings with the researcher.</u> These meetings--2 per week--will take approx. 30-45 minutes, depending on the work to be discussed. Meeting times will be arranged at <u>your convenience</u>, preferably on Mondays and Thursdays, or Tuesdays and Fridays, for the period of the course (today through July 3). We'll have a follow-up meeting if needed later

WHAT WILL THE PROCEDURE BE?

    At the end of class on the days we decide to meet, you will submit to me any writing you've done in relation to Spaceship Earth since our last meeting. Writing will be duplicated and returned to you when we meet. (Exams and quizzes will be handled separately) We will meet in my office, 237 Bartlett Hall (top floor, East wing), unless another location is more convenient for you.

FIGURE 2 (CONT.)

WILL PARTICIPATION IN THIS STUDY AFFECT MY GRADE FOR THIS COURSE?

No. Your identity will not be disclosed to your instructor.

HOW CAN PARTICIPATION HELP ME?

You may find that sharing your work on a regular basis with an impartial outsider provides incentive. Although I will not evaluate your writing, our conversations about your experience in this class may help you clarify your thoughts about the course and the work you are doing for it. You may also like to have a role in research that could have an impact on writing assignments you will encounter at UNI.

INTERESTED?   SEE BACK

I AM INTERESTED IN PARTICIPATING IN A STUDY OF THE JOURNAL ASSIGNMENT IN EARTH SCIENCE 87: 036, SPACESHIP EARTH. I understand that my participation in this study is voluntary, that all material pertaining to my participation will remain confidential and that my identity will not be disclosed in any publication related to this study.

NAME_____   CLASS (please circle one) FR SOPH JR SR

Phone #_____

Best time to contact me_____

Please return to Anne Johnstone, 237 Bartlett Hall. If you need more information, I'll be glad to talk to you after class today.   I can be reached this afternoon at my office numbers, 273-2346 or -3489. Evening phone: 266-7791.

seemed, like the expectations I described, likely to attract students who wanted to do well in the course. I intended to influence their work in this class as little as possible, but I understood that people cooperate in research when they anticipate some gain by doing so.

In classroom research, incentives to participate may be intangible; Florio and Clark's (1982) ethnography suggests that attention and approval from sympathetic adults makes cooperative informants of children. On the other hand, North's (1986a) study of journal keepers in a philosophy class suggests that college students like to be paid for their time. I considered offering money in exchange for cooperation, but decided to make incentives that were more explicitly related to participants' potential success as writers and students, in this class and elsewhere in their college careers. To appeal to students' interest in having an influence on their teachers, I said, "You might want to be a part of a project that could have an effect on how writing is assigned in gen. ed. courses." To relate this appeal to "Spaceship Earth," I went on to say that "You might find that talking to me about what you're doing in this course would help you study or retain more of what you're learning—at least it will give you a chance to express your feelings about this class and what you're doing in it."

The four students who were to become my informants—Beth, Tina, Jim, and Jill—had their own reasons for wanting to talk to me about themselves and their writing, but they all intended, as least initially, to be good students in "Spaceship Earth." That they all wanted to get as much as they could from the class obviously influenced what they did in it, what they chose to tell me in our conversations, and, ultimately, the way I interpreted their work.

At the end of the first class period, five students left word that they wanted to participate. One of them told me the next period that she wouldn't have time; the other four agreed to let me duplicate all their writing for "Spaceship Earth" twice a week, and, on those days, to meet individually with me. My student informants' conversations with me about their writing and about their experience of this class offered me insight into the direction of this research, which I will discuss in "Interviewing Informants," below.

The presentation I made to the class on its first meeting would affect not only my informants' subsequent relationships with me, but my subsequent behaviors and roles in attending class meetings. I had told Professor Weber that I would be "auditing" the class. I turn next to what that meant for my behavior and for others' responses to me.

Collecting Data

Observing/Participating in Class   I chose to attend "Spaceship Earth" class meetings because I wanted to find out what connection there might be between what happened in class and what happened in the journal entries. As I've indicated, I intended to be unobtrusive in observing what happened in "Spaceship Earth." I wanted, in so far as possible, to experience this class as a student would. Like the 15 students who received academic credit for the course, I spent most of the class hours quietly listening to and recording the kind of information that would serve my purposes in being there. However, I chose not to be completely silent before and during the class meeting time, so I could build rapport with my informants and follow up the interest in environmental issues that led me to choose this class as a research site. Although a transcript of the 40 total hours of "Spaceship Earth" class shows my voice for less than one of them, my participation, like that of any other member of this community, influenced what others said, did, and wrote. My questions for or responses to Weber and my conversations with other students before or after class affected the agenda and the dynamics of interaction in the class. My roles in responding to my informants during class affected theirs in responding to me.

Like my informants, I responded to Weber and to "Spaceship Earth" students much as an interested student might. I participated in class—asked questions of Weber or responded to his questions, that is—12 times, less often than three of my informants participated, but more often than did most of the other students. I had introduced myself to the class as a researcher, but by coming to class every meeting, dressing like other students, sitting with them and asking of "our" professor the same kinds of questions they did, I encouraged class participants to respond to me, in part, as a fellow student. Before class or in the hallway or restroom during class breaks, others talked to me about Weber or their classmates, complained about tests or the amount of reading they had to do, or asked what I though he was going to be looking for on the next exam.

During class, as others did, I asked Weber at least six times to clarify or elaborate on material he was presenting to the group, doing so when he paused or when he asked if there were any questions. For example, I asked Weber about procedural matters (what we would do about a field trip if it rained); about cosmological or geological processes (whether "Steady State" was an accepted cosmological theory, why "pillow lava is shaped that way," and how the "mercalli scale" was determined); about his proposal for a local hazardous waste facility; and, twice, about how to interpret diagrams he projected. By participating in class in these ways, I responded to Professor Weber as my student informants told me they did: I asked him questions when I thought others might share my curiosity or uncertainty about his topics.

Nonetheless, because I had presented myself as a researcher, didn't get grades on the tests, and didn't participate in an in-class debate on nuclear energy, it was clear to those taking this course for credit that I wasn't a registered student. If my responses to Weber were studentlike, they also conveyed the message that I was Weber's peer. I showed the class that I was comfortable with Weber on the two or three occasions when I made joking rejoinders to his comments. In referring to him by first name, I may have encouraged others to do likewise; having heard Weber say that he wanted this to be an informal class, two of my informants, Beth and Jim (both nontraditional students), called him by first name during class, and in their journal entries, after I had done so. My respectful but genial manner of responding to Weber may also have provided an etiquette model that encouraged others to save expressions of frustration or anger for their journal entries.

My questions and comments for Weber, like those of other students, served to support his agenda for this lecture/demonstration class, and thereby, as I will argue in Chapter 3, support the agendas of journal entries. Approximately 90 percent of all talk was initiated by Weber. Review of my questions and comments shows that they encouraged Weber to defend, elaborate, clarify, or otherwise carry on with his narrative or explanatory presentation. For example, in responding to Weber's "Anybody got any good stories?" with, "That's your department, Carl," I encouraged Weber to entertain the group. Or, in asking this question (to which I knew the answer): "Aren't mudslides an important volcanic hazard?" to which Weber responded, "Oh, I'm glad you brought that up," I encouraged him to complete the "Volcanic Hazards" outline that served as the basis for his presentation to the class that day.

My behavior in response to class members also advanced Weber's goals for group activities that were addressed in the journal entries. During preparations for an in-class debate that Weber had enthusiastically organized, I briefly acted as coach to one of the teams: the transcript shows that, shortly before Weber entered the room where this group was meeting, I asked if they had considered an argument not yet mentioned. Because someone had, I don't know whether my question made a difference in this team's performance or in subsequent journal comments on the debate. However, during another group activity, a comment I made guided how others subsequently commented and seems likely to have influenced journal entries on this subject. In this case, Weber asked students to share responses to a question—"What is the significance of the common, ordinary light bulb?"—that he had asked them, during class, to answer in their journals. In-class writing and follow-up discussion activities were new to the class, and in the silence which followed Weber's call for responses, I offered an answer first. Having discussed this exercise with Weber, I was predisposed to give the kind of response he was expecting, and he returned later to my point, elaborating on it before ending class with a reminder that the in-class writing should be continued in the journals. Of the ten students who continued writing about the in-class topic in their journals, seven responded to the topic as I had.

Thus I probably influenced what other students said in class and wrote in their journals about this activity. The transcript suggests that as class participant observer, I behaved as an interested student, while my effect on others' behaviors tended to support Weber's plans. In responding to my informants during class, I enacted a number of differing roles which affected theirs in responding to me. Transcripts of my interviews and conversations with Beth, Tina, Jim, and Jill show that they understood me in part as an authority, in part as an "objective" observer, and in part as their peer.

Having been introduced to the class as a professional, and having introduced myself in a manner that suggested I regarded Weber as a peer, I was perceived as an authority, not simply on writing, but on topics Weber presented to the class. During our interview meetings, Beth and Jim asked my opinion not only of the way they had written entries, but of subjects they were considering in their journals. I tried in class to ask questions that other students might have had, but (unlike the others, having nothing to lose by asking them), I could do so with a confidence and ease which apparently suggested to my informants, until I told them otherwise, that I knew more about geology than they did. Although, for example, I gave no indication that I was privy to Weber's plans for testing the class on mineral and rock origins, Beth and Tina assumed that I knew correct answers to their first exam.

Nonetheless, for at least one informant, my authoritative and teacherly roles co-existed with my role as her peer. I often sat next to or near Beth, a nontraditional student with whom I traded anecdotes about current events or people in the local news. On one occasion, sitting next to Beth, I shared with her my responses to an in-class geography exercise involving place locations. Although Beth might have perceived me then as a kind of surrogate teacher, or a tutor sitting in for Weber (who was out of the room), I was later proved wrong on a couple of points and was thus shown to be a student vis à vis this exercise. The transcript also shows that, as Weber introduced the topic of sanitary landfills to the class one day near the middle of the course, Beth and I joked about his comments in conversation with each other. In this instance my response to Beth reinforced my role as a fellow critic of our instructor; she was thereby encouraged during our interviews to criticize Weber's performance.

In this section, I have suggested that my observing and participating in "Spaceship Earth" affected its agenda, its dynamics, and the relationships I initiated with my student informants. These relationships developed in biweekly or weekly interview meetings. My purpose in conducting these meetings was to learn as much as Beth, Tina, Jill, and Jim would tell me about how, when, where, why, and for whom they wrote entries in their "Spaceship Earth" journals. My questions for and responses to informants, and theirs for me, were influenced by my choice to observe and participate in class and the roles I had taken in doing so; what my informants told me in our interview meetings in turn influenced my interpretation of their writing. In the next section, I describe these meetings, suggesting how my interview plans were affected by my informants' responses to me; how, in turn, my responses to informants affected their journal keeping; and how these interviews refined my research questions and the scope of my inquiry.

Interviewing Informants In early June, 1986, as I prepared to conduct interviews with student informants, my plans were these: for the four-week period of the course I would meet twice a week, for perhaps a half hour, with each student. One follow-up meeting would be needed after the course ended. At the end of the class period before we were to meet, I would collect my informants' journals, notes, and any other writing (e.g., exams or quizzes); I would duplicate this material, returning it during an afternoon meeting time. At our first meeting, I planned to ask for information I could use to develop profiles of each informant's history as a student, a writer, and a journal or diary keeper. In subsequent meetings, I planned to discuss the duplicated writing, annotated with my questions about its intended audience(s), purposes, and style (that is, organization and language). To gather information about my informants' processes in writing, I also considered asking them to compose aloud or to let me observe them write entries.

These plans were modified somewhat by my informants' schedules and interests and by the often unpredicted direction of our conversations. Having anticipated a total of 38 half-hour meetings (36 with student informants; two with their instructor), I actually conducted 26 typically 45- to 60-minute meetings (four with Weber, seven with Tina and Beth, ten with Jill, and eight with Jim). I abandoned plans to collect compose-aloud transcripts or to watch my informants as they wrote; none of them was particularly enthusiastic about my doing so. Neither was I, as I realized such activities would seem intrusive, at odds with my interest in observing behaviors as they naturally occur.

The first meetings were the most like interviews; they were the most structured by my planned questions (Figure 3) on the informants' backgrounds in writing and their histories as students. I had also planned questions on their experiences as journal keepers and their first impressions of "Spaceship Earth," but my informants' willingness to talk about their histories as students and writers, prompted by my interest in hearing them do so, meant that conversation about journal keeping was postponed until our second meeting.

For the most part, my plan to duplicate and annotate writing worked pretty well, but Jim could only meet with me before class, and I was sometimes unable to photocopy his work before we met. Twice Beth didn't have her journal with her during class, and since she lived too far from campus to retrieve it conveniently, we talked, as we often did, about her perception of class dynamics, her writing, and other matters of shared interest. Jill and Tina always had their journals and notes ready for me to duplicate and read before we met.

FIGURE 3

QUESTIONS FOR INFORMANTS

1. Home/School background

   where did you grow up?
   is that where you went to high school?
   what did you do after high school?
   why did you decide to attend UNI?
   has your college experience been what you expected?
   what are the best classes you've taken? the worst?
   what classes are you taking this summer?

2. writing background:

   first memory of writing?
   do you remember how old you were when you learned to write?
   did people you lived with do much writing? what kind?
   do you remember what kind of reaction you got to your
   writing?
   how old were you when you learned to read?
   did people in your home do much reading? What?
   what did you like to read?
   did people read to you?
   what kind of writing do you remember doing in elementary
   school? junior high?
   high school? Any composition classes? term papers?
   any particular memories of a writing project you worked on?
   journal keeping: have you ever kept a journal or diary?
   did anyone you know keep one?
   what kinds of things did you write in it?
   how long did/have you written in it?
   has anyone else ever read any part of it? why do you write
   in it?
   has anyone else ever read it?
   have you ever kept one for a class? How did that turn out?

3. Spaceship Earth assignments/dynamics

   why are you taking S.E. this summer?
   what was your first impression of this class?
   of Professor Weber? of other students?
   what did you expect when you registered for it?
   is it like other courses you've taken here?
   what do you think is Weber's purpose in assigning a journal?
   if you had to describe this assignment to someone who missed
   class today, how would you go about it?
   if you didn't have to turn it in, would you do it?
   will this journal be like any other journal you've kept?
   how do you think this journal will be different?
   do you have any questions about the assignment?

I was usually able to annotate my informants' material before our meetings. As I read, I marked grammatical, lexical, and topical features of the writing that I wanted to ask about. (See Figure 4 for samples of annotated journal entries.) Interested in my informants' sense of the audience(s) for their entries, I asked, for example, if a *you* in the text meant Weber, me, the writer, or a general reader. I sometimes asked informants if they would change anything in a particular entry if it were to be graded. Most of my questions, however, were about the sources of journal entries. Or they were open-ended requests for elaboration: "What do you have in mind here?" "Is this from a news article?" "Meaning?" or "What brought this to mind?" Although I had decided not to collect compose-aloud protocols, I asked a number of questions about how entries were composed. Jim had conducted a clinical psychology research project, and he expected, I think, that I wanted quantifiable data. He seemed eager to recollect his "thought process" in drafting; to show me, that is, where he had paused, and how "key words" had helped him organize sentences as he wrote them. Tina offered me detailed information about how she had planned and, in some places, edited entries so as to "explain [her]self" to her readers clearly and accurately.

Although I prepared notes of what I planned to ask about the journal or class activities for each interview, the agenda for our meetings was negotiated by my informants' as well as my own interests. For example, when I met with Beth on the afternoon after the first exam for the course, the transcript shows that she responded to my questions about the journal entries with references to the exam. After asking her what she had missed on the test, I used her defense of an answer to "return to something you said in your journal, a question you raised in the beginning about your difficulty comprehending an infinite." Beth briefly elaborated on the cosmological subject of this entry (about how intergalactic space is measured), expressing disappointment that Weber hadn't asked about the "red shift" on the test. I then tried to steer her back to journal writing, but Beth responded with "one clarification thing" about her behavior during our earlier meeting. The "clarification thing," related to her history as a student and writer, was part of the information I used to develop a profile that helped me understand the roles that Beth seemed to express in her journal entries.

After the first interview, our conversations typically began with my asking informants about what I guessed they might have

FIGURE 4   Annotated Sample, Journal Entry
_____

6/18

Last night, as I sat on the porch observing
a thunderstorm approach I couldn't help
but feel a sense of excitement. The beauty of
heard
tornado
the dark clouds reflected in the backdrop
against jagged lightening bolts, and the   *drop*
sound of thunder indicating the magnitude of
the storm.

But then I always get excited at the forecast
of a heavy snow, or a tornado warning, or
how so?
a blizzard about to blanket the region. What
may be more excentric, is that I have to
experience these events by exposing myself
to these elements for the immediate thrill,
and sense of danger that accompanies
these storms.

I think Freud was right when he began
to understand that humans are driven by
what
are
these?
the Life Force and the Death Force, with the
superego of our personalities mediating the
two. And when I stand in the midst of a blizzard
or facing a heavy black sky I feel I can
empathize with

FIGURE 4 (CONT.)   Annotated Sample, Journal Entry

Model

Spaceship Earth Journal

June 9, 1986

I tried to write her "exp. of as a reader" pres. kid.?

[We have barely scratched the surface of the information available in this class and already we have a million questions forming in my mind.]

meaning?

[The "big bang" theory is a form of logic I cannot identify with at this stage.]

why not

seg. only in 6.13 conv.

[Maybe I will change my mind by the end of the four weeks when more supporting data has been absorbed. I really am to uninformed now to make a knowledge statement of my own belief or non-belief in the theory.] [The haunting questions are 1. Where did the original mass come from? + 2. If there is an end to our universe — what next? To imagine an infinite nothingness staggers my mind.]

don't know just what LB expects — her "uniformed" opinion — might be indivd.

elaborates 6.13

"journal is different than most people think" p. 5 6.13   conv. 6.13

dif. between personal + academic opinion

found of particular interest in the day's class, or in current events pertinent to geological issues. For example, I began my second conversation with Tina, a physics major, by asking what she thought of Weber's explanation of seismic waves ("good," but "nothing new," she said). Jim had formerly managed a railroad-car cleaning company that illegally dumped toxic wastes. We began two of our meetings with conversation about local news stories of high arsenic levels in groundwater downriver from a local chemical company. When I asked Jill, a younger and more traditional college sophomore (planning to major in home economics) about her first impressions of the class, she described her reaction to the size, shape, and color of the classroom, and she mentioned she had noticed that "all the boys sit in the back." So I asked her, to begin our second meeting, if she had any idea why they did. ("Maybe they're used to doing that," she said.) In subsequent meetings, I asked Jill for her reaction to who was sitting where (the sexes had begun to integrate), because she had gotten to know about half of the class. My conversations with Beth, with whom I talked the longest and about the widest range of subjects, often began with her clarifying something she had mentioned earlier or explaining what she had been doing since we last talked. Of the four students, Jill and Beth needed the least prompting to talk, Jill in part because she felt pressured by her father (a university professor) to do well in this and all her classes, and she seemed to value the chance to air her frustrations. Beth, like Jim an older and nontraditional student, had "the gift of gab," as she put it. I looked forward to conversations with Beth, not only for what she could tell me about the sources of her journal entries and her view of "Spaceship Earth" dynamics, but also because she told me Eudora Welty-like stories of her life in rural Independence, Iowa.

If my plans were affected by my informants' interests, their journal writing was also affected by their meetings with me. All of my informants indicated that they were motivated by our conversations to, as Jim put it, "try a little bit more," or as Tina said, "put more effort" into journal writing. When I asked Tina if she would do anything differently in her journal if I weren't reading it, she said, "I'd think less about it; I'd just do it [and] get it over with." When we first met, Jill said, "I'll probably want to do a good job on [the journal]," suggesting that our conversations added to her incentive to write the entries so as to satisfy what she understood to be my and her instructor's, as well as her own expectations.

Not only their attitude toward the writing, but the time of day and days of the week when Beth, Tina, and Jim wrote journal entries were influenced by their talking to me about their entries. For the first two weeks of class, they wrote entries on the dates shown in their journals, but thereafter they used their appointment times with me as incentive to get caught up, writing entries for days they hadn't done so on the days we were scheduled to meet. Beth not only wanted to be caught up when we met, but she wanted to be able to give me entries that represented her "best effort." When the course began, her work schedule left her very little time for journal writing; within ten days of our first meeting, she gave up some of her work hours, leaving herself a little more time on the nights before we had planned to meet.

I phrased questions (as did Odell and Goswami, 1982) so as to indicate that I did not intend to evaluate my informants' writing, but that I was interested in learning why they had chosen to write what they did. Nonetheless, the transcript record and journal entries suggest that my questions and comments affected my informants' rhetorical and stylistic choices in writing. After changing her work hours so as to be able to "put more concerted effort into [journal writing]," Beth on June 20 told me, about her journal entries of June 19 and 20, that "I tried to write with a feverish pitch . . . because you . . . commented the other day on how small [the earlier entries were]." When I asked, "Are you saying these two [entries] are more complete?" she responded, "Well, one question leads to another." During this interview, I asked Beth about a shift in the tone of an entry she had written after the second test. The first sentence of this entry expresses anger and frustration; the second gives an abstract generalization about the value of being wrong. I said, "This sentence doesn't sound like you—the one before it is personal and emotional and this one is more abstract—sounds almost like you're writing a memo or something." Beth's response to me suggested that she fashioned this sentence to accommodate her perception of my expectations: "If I weren't giving this to you or Weber," she said, "I would have written 'I'm going to try to remember why I screwed up so I won't do that again,' but as you can see I got tired of . . . trying to think things through too fast . . . as I was doing."

If Beth got the message from my asking her about the length of her entries that they weren't long or reflective enough, Jill responded to a question I asked her about usage in a way that suggested she took it as evaluative. I had asked her several questions about her perception of the audience to a letterlike entry that began "Hi again" and concluded "As you can see. . . ." Jill responded by comparing this entry to a letter. But then she said, "I'll know not to use the 'you' I suppose!" Although I urged her "[not] to do anything different" on my account, in none of her subsequent entries did Jill use the second person to refer to herself.

If Beth's and Jill's perceptions of my expectations affected the way they referred to themselves or their experience in the journals, Tina's perception of what I might need to know about the context of information she referred to in her entries may have affected the vocabulary she used and the extent to which she developed some entries. When I asked her, for example, whether the first sentence of her journal summary of a *Science News* article (she had written "first some background information") referred to what she already knew or to background material presented in the article, she responded, "No, that was basically in the article. I already knew that. . . . And then I put that in there for the reader, so they understood it." "The reader?" I asked. "Well, you and Weber."

Answers to questions about my informants' sense of whom they were writing for suggested to me that they were using their developing understanding of Weber's expectations in attempts to communicate with him. Reading some of my informants' early entries as letterlike (Jill began a couple of entries with "hi"; Tina appended a "PS") suggested that a theory of "cooperativeness" in conversation that I was reading about could be applied to these texts, explaining their rhetoric. I was to find, as I explain in the final section of this chapter, that this theory was inappropriate to my purposes, but my hypothesis (that journal keeping represented a kind of communication) directed the questions I asked informants and the way I was ultimately to read their texts.

Inscribing

As North (1987) points out, by "inscribing" (or writing down) what they see and hear in field notes or other records, researchers begin to construct the "alternative imaginative universe" that an ethnography of writing represents. Nonetheless, accounts of data collection and inscription are not typically included in published composition ethnographies. This may be because the process of investigation and the product of investigation—the analysis of written texts—are assumed to be separable. This study, however, assumes that process and product are continuous and, as I've argued, reflexive. Because my interpretation of written texts focuses on the social context of their composition and use, the way I collected them is part of what defines that context and is thus integral to the findings of this research.

Tape-recording Audio recordings of my observation and participation in "Spaceship Earth" and of my interviews with informants were crucial to the development of my interpretation of writing in this class. Without detailed records of who said what, when, and to whom, I might not have been inclined or been able to see that writing and talking in this class affected each other. Tape-recording also allowed me to participate in class meetings and conduct interviews in the ways I've described. Taping the interviews freed me to make notes on my duplicates of informants' texts, without fear of losing the "off paper" talk that would shape my interpretation of the writing we talked about. Taping in class freed me to take the notes about writing and nonverbal behaviors that I will describe shortly.

Nonetheless, this way of collecting data, like all the activities of this research was, as North (1987) puts it, a "compromise between what the investigator might like to know and what, in terms of intrusiveness, it will cost her to find out" (p. 295). The price for making tape-recordings was the extent to which the recorder's presence influenced people's behavior. To minimize intrusiveness, I used a pocket-sized recorder; here the trade-off was that it lacked the range of a larger, more sensitive machine. Thus in class I could access clearly only the talk among students sitting near me.

To insure that I'd have as complete a transcript as possible, I brought the tape-recorder with me to all but one of the classes, a field trip. Since I had the recorder with me at all the regular lecture room meetings, I don't know how it may have influenced the proceedings. (Differences between the interaction among Weber and his students during the field trip and during regular class meetings could be attributed to differences in meeting places and agendas.) Although my research neither confirms nor denies Douglas' claim (cited in Bogdan & Taylor, 1984) that recording devices have fundamental effects on the behavior of research subjects, my taping was nonetheless of use to at least one student, who borrowed some of my cassettes before a test. Dixie's performance on the test then—and her subsequent behavior in class— may have been influenced by my tapes.

In the one-to-one interview situation, the tape-recorder's presence was more obvious than it was in the classroom; twice I needed to turn it off for Weber to feel comfortable revealing information (about his tenure review hearing) that I would use to understand political constraints on his writing assignments. My failure to tell Beth that our first conversation was being taped might have cost me her confidence, had she not evidently needed the opportunity I gave her to express herself. Although I had assured my informants that the confidentiality of our conversations would be protected, none—with Beth's exception—was explicitly critical of journal keeping while talking "for the record."

Notetaking   Used to supplement and cross-check audio-tapes, my notetaking during interviews with informants helped me develop the profiles that I used in interpreting their writing, and my notes about class meetings helped me understand how writing and talking interacted with each other in class. Jotted during or after interviews, my notes about my informants' histories as students and journal keepers helped me interpret the writing we talked about. When I considered, for example, why Tina had summarized *Science News* articles in almost half of her journal entries, my note that she had "back issues 'lying around the house'" suggested a reason. Or my note that Beth "became emotionally upset when I mentioned [Professor X]" led us in the next meeting to a conversation about her sensitivity to the way former teachers had treated her writing. This piece of information suggested a reason that journal keeping proved difficult for her.

As a cross-check to tapes of class meetings, my notes turned out to be crucial: about three of 40 total hours of class meeting tapes were accidently erased while they were being transcribed. As I will illustrate, my notes strengthened my understanding that writing worked in collaboration with talk, structuring and reinforcing what was said, what would be said, and what could be said. This understanding led me to read the journals as agencies for the development of relationships that were initiated conjointly by writing and talking.

The information I took from class not only affected, but was affected by my informants, whom I usually sat next to or near. Where I sat also influenced what I was likely to hear and see. On the sixth day of class, when Weber asked how the "journals [were] going," nobody reacted verbally. But the student sitting next to me flipped his hand back and forth in a "so-so" gesture. With this response to Weber's question and other information about class dynamics that I describe shortly, I speculated that ambivalent or hostile comments about journal keeping would be reserved for the journal entries themselves. With evidence in my informants' journals that this was so, I hypothesized that journal keeping provided students an opportunity to vent frustrations that could not appropriately be expressed in class.

My notes about the first class period (Figure 5) are something of a hodgepodge, but for the most part, they identify what couldn't be audio-recorded: dimensions of the classroom and descriptions of what it contained, brief physical descriptions of students and instructor, and identification of what was written on the blackboard or shown on an overhead projector. On the third day of class, June 11, I realized that if I was going to represent accurately what was on the blackboard, I needed to reorient my note-taking on the page, using the two sides of the 8 1/2 x 11 pad as top and bottom. I still needed more space to accommodate what was written on the board, so I made a tablet of unlined 8 1/2 x 17 paper, which I quartered to represent the four-sectioned blackboard. My making this change was later to affect how I could interpret and use what I had noted. Because one or two sections of my tablet "blackboard" were now often blank (Weber typically used the middle two sections), I had space to note accompanying talk, some of it transcribed later from audiotapes. (See Figure 6 for a sample of these annotated class notes.) Because I was thus able to see how blackboard or projected writing and drawing was used to anticipate, rehearse, elaborate, or otherwise assist talking, I hypothesized that journal writing might similarly be related to talk with its intended reader.

My representation of blackboard and other projected material formed a backdrop for notes of talk that explicitly pertained to class dynamics or that otherwise struck me as illustrative of the particular style and aims of the speaker. In the margins of my tablet, for example, I noted nonverbal aspects of Weber's performance as a lecturer ("[CW] makes sound of race car 'zipping by'"); quoted some of his glosses on his own performance ("long way from story I'm trying to tell"), or on the conduct of this class ("because this course isn't a pre-requisite for anything, we can go off on a tangent if we want"); commented on patterns ("3rd ref. to Carl Sagan"); or roughly transcribed words or usages that seemed to be characteristic of Weber's western Pennsylvania dialect: ("fizz its," [for "physics"]; "If I 'leave go' of this book").

Because I wanted to understand writing in the context of interaction among students and professor, I noted what I could of what

FIGURE 5   Sample Class Notes, June 9, 1986

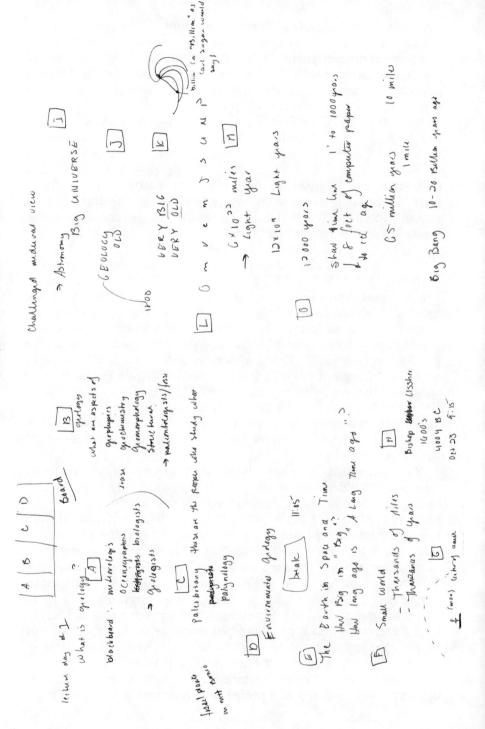

Challenged medieval view

→ Astronomy

Big UNIVERSE

GEOLOGY
OLD

1800

VERY BIG
VERY OLD

O m n v e m s u n ?

Billion (as "Brillion" as
Carl Sagan would
say)

O m n v e m s u n

6 × 10²³ miles
→ light
year

C1 × 10⁶
Light years

12 000 years

Shoe time line   1' to 1000 yrs
1 8 feet of computer paper
the cal. age

6.5 million years   10 miles

1 mile

Big Bang   10-20 Billion years ago

Lecture day #1

What is Geology?

A	B	C	D

Board

B
geology
what am aspects of

A

blackboard : meteorologists

Oceanographers
biophysists biologists   ivox
→ geologists

geophysics
geochemistry
geomorphology
structure
→ paleontologists/fossil

C

Paleobotany   these are the people who study what
paleozoic
palynology

total place
on next frame

D   Environmental Geology

break   11:05

E   The Earth in Space and Time
How big is "Big"?
How long ago is A Long Time ago "...?

F   Small world
- Thousands of Miles
- Thousands of years

H
Bishop Usher Usshes
1600's
4004 BC
O23   6:15

G   (was) century week

FIGURE 5 (CONT.) Sample Class Notes, June 9, 1986

pressed play, key mistake — how did course get its name? Spaceship Earth — E.S. 87:036 — G. 9 — Baker 166 off.

physical geo — 9:50

McCollum Science Hall 1536

bay I — day I

room — 17 students

~~15 — 16~~

(18) 17 [illegible] 12 × 12 — 5 rows seats

30

CB enthusiastic, cheerful — red tie, brown slacks, checked shirt

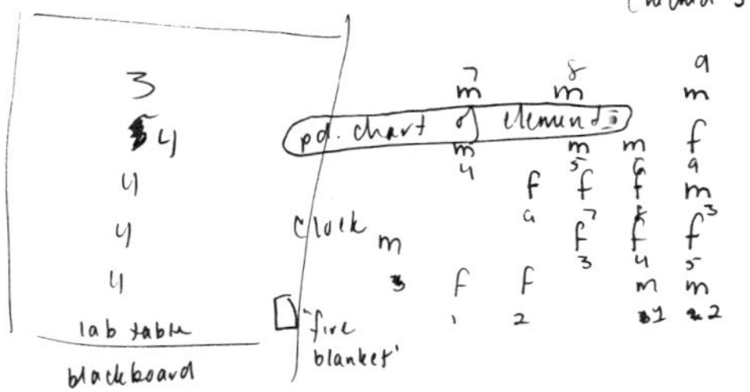

3
4
4
4
4
lab table
blackboard
pd. chart of elements
clock
"fire blanket"

f 1 older student
2 orange jacket, blonde
m 1 blonde, glasses, had phys geog
m 2 green tee shirt brunette brown eyes
f 3 brunette older freckled
f 4 blonde
f 5 feather - red head · plaid
m 3 blonde: short hair
f 6 dark blonde, puffed up hair, glasses
f 7 lt blonde. blue tinted glasses
f 8 dark blonde

m 3 ruddy complexion, dark blond
f 9 dk blonde / blue eyes
m 7 blonde, close cropped hair
m 8 brunette
m 9 blonde: t shirt

Journal assign: · handout
- CB held up old journals
- samples, overhead proj.

(1) Journal examples Jan 85 — Lecture topic: gross Structure of the Universe

The most amazing thing isn't the numbers or time involved because I can't imagine . . .

(2) Thoughts about: Lecture notes about the crust.

I know that I take a lot of the "facts" you give us for granted, but the ocean crust being younger

(3) Plate tectonics

Boy am I glad you didn't see my hand go up

(4) After the test

(5) (another writer) "religious significance" I must say that I cannot comprehend how

(6) first test in this class: emotional response - anger

FIGURE 6 Sample Annotated Class Notes, June 24, 1986

Day #12 6/24

what's the source of flooding?
Source of rain?
Will excessive rain dam failure?

is often
off ten
gaush

B + MB: Conversation about Photography
Well I bought my Lucia
overhawed
B: photo flowers
very detailed
LB: Pintay
Solosan

who was wasn't
here yesterday?
So don't anybody discuss
even or ask me any
questions about it because ⊛
were got somebody who
hasn't taken it yet

We were somewhere in the
middle of a flood yesterday
+ to make this somewhat
more realistic I'm going to
turn off the heater + leave it ⊛

5. Interbasin transfer
6. Consumptive uses
7. Evaporation
8. Plant use — "crazy idea to kill aspens to save H2O"

Sigue from about
John: Robin Hood + caroline
Little John ★

we have contraries of
ux of n universes of
terms name we name
def of out of
no way

Flow= discharge
CFS = cubic ft/sec
m³ sec
M³/sec

Stage 14ft

GAGING STATION
measurement / sis nal
LB interested in this measurement text

another word uni lots like John
John looks like little John

Amount
1. Release from Dams
2. Melting snow
3. Ground water
4. Direct/Near Direct Runoff

A. Saturation of Soil
B. Vegetation
C. Slope
D. Soil Conditions (frozen)
E. Intensity
F. Amount of Rain
G. Duration
H. Land Use

Why are hundred yrs?

Flash Flood
smaller basins
single storms

Riverine Floods
Small/basins
big

Record
100 yr Flood
recurrence interval
May last for months

Overhead Diagram of a gaging station
and
rating curve

Hydrograph Marel of flows
stage over him

Break
B: you haven't had
a John for any while
C: I don't have
a more either

students said to, or asked, Weber. I paid particular attention to my informants' comments, for reference in our interviews later during the day. My notes of what students said and how much they spoke helped me to understand what they regarded as sayable in "Spaceship Earth." Weber often seemed to urge students to participate in class, and, with jokes, lighthearted asides, anecdotes from his own experience, and a generally easygoing manner, he seemed to be encouraging an informal atmosphere. Nonetheless, students talked to Weber during class far less than he did to them. Fewer than half of the 17 students ever talked to Weber during class, and almost all of what students said took the form of questions for him or responses to his questions. Combined with evidence that students tried to communicate with Weber in their journals, my notes that students hesitated to express themselves to Weber during class supported the hypothesis that journal keeping provided an outlet for what couldn't appropriately be said in class.

Interpreting Journal Keeping in "Spaceship Earth"

A circuitous route took me from notes about class activities, informant interviews, and collection of journal texts to the understanding of their interconnection which I discuss in subsequent chapters of this work. My progress toward developing an interpretation of the material I had collected was checked, in a sense, by my interest in using this material to test preexisting frameworks for interpreting journals or analyzing communication, and thus "ground" my research before it had made full use of my text, interview, and class data. On the other hand, my exploration of conceptual sorting ideas drawn from investigations of journal keeping in other college classes, from a sociolinguistic theory of conversation, and from a rhetorical theory of "intertextual" relations helped me to recast and focus the three broad questions with which I had begun this study. First, as I considered North's idea that journal entries expressed their authors' positions within the discipline of philosophy (and Herrington's idea that writing in chemistry classes expressed disciplinary formal conventions), I began to see that "learning" in the journals could be recast as assimilating the conventions of a particular community. Second, as I considered that H. P. Grice's (1975) ideas about how speakers communicate with each other might apply to my material, it dawned on me that my question about how the journal writers conceived their audiences could be recast as a question about how they chose to present and express themselves to their reader(s). Third, when I considered what the texts might have in common, trying unsuccessfully to use Culler's (1981) notion of rhetorical *presupposition* in doing so, I realized that I could use information about my informants' prior histories to suggest they were predisposed to take certain roles in responding to each other.

Categorizing "Spaceship Earth" Activities   As I collected information about what was happening in class, I was also beginning to interpret what I had heard, seen, and noted. Almost every day while the class was in session and at various times throughout the next three months (August through October of 1986), I made entries in a journal kept as a kind of sketchbook of my ideas for making sense of this class and the writing I was collecting from it. This journal began with my impressions of class activities. In the first six entries, I used this journal to organize class activities by categorizing them.

Under the heading "Day #1," I put activities into two categories: "demos" and "drawing." These expanded in the second day's entry, becoming "photo," "demo[s]," "pictures on board," "charts on board," "drawings," "calculations," "misc.," and "questions from class." On the third day, these categories were "transparencies," "personal experience anecdote," "pun," "illustrations," "demonstrations," "tables," "drawings," "questions to class," and "questions from class."

While the first two entries were primarily concerned with categories of activities the instructor engaged in, the second through sixth included questions that students asked and my impressions of students' behaviors or attitudes. (In preparation for an interview with Weber, I also used the journal to note "questions for [CW].") On the fourth day, when the class went on a field trip (to look at rocks in a local cemetery), my entry had two parts, the first titled "questions," the second "demo." In the questions part, I named question-askers and, from my class notes, recopied what they had asked. I wanted to remember my informants' questions, for reference in our conversations, and for use in developing a picture of who said what in class.

On the fifth day, unlike the preceding four because it required all students to participate by taking a test, I was interested by a change I sensed in the atmosphere of the class: "people nervous," I noted. "No questions/restlessness." Because this was an exam day and because my seatmate had commented on the way I was taking notes "in column" (as debaters do, he said), I was moved to reflect on "the irony . . . that in taking notes this way—trying just to replicate what [CW] puts on the board—I'm not learning as I would if I put the ideas in my own language." My observation about how I was learning would lead me to reflect on what "learning" seemed to mean thus far for the class as a whole.

Reflecting, Analyzing, Evaluating   On the sixth and seventh days of class, I wrote at greater length, involved in the recursive and interrelated processes of reflecting, analyzing, and evaluating that characterize interpretation (Goetz & LeCompte, 1984; North, 1987). After "summarizing" the sixth class I wrote, "what I've learned so far." I commented here on my interest in "people's backgrounds" and went on to note that "information about writing habits in this class interesting in light of prior histories." Then I made a note to myself about the mechanics of data collection ("have to take different kind of notes") and ended up by synthesizing what informants had told me and what I'd observed in a comment on teaching technique: "Demonstrations make material 'real' for people."

My entry for the next day, June 17, also begins with a brief description of that day's class: "Demonstrations today: slinky, paint stick slingshot" and on one of my informants: "Beth apologizing for her questions: 'just one more'." This entry, however, goes on to name and reflect on class dynamics:

> I've been thinking about how this class is "traditional." The presentation is through lecture demonstration and illustration. The class sits facing the teacher, who gives information. Students ask questions which prompt more explanation or illustration. When students say something, it is usually to amplify, not to challenge. [CW] says "yesterday we discussed," but actually there was no discussion, if by discussion is meant the exchange of information. Does *he* learn anything? I'll have to ask.

I went on to consider whether a community of any kind was developing in this class:

> Are the students being drawn into some kind of community? A community that their teacher seems to have much more influence on than they do. [CW] seems at some level to be-

lieve SE is a community when he says "we discussed" but the students don't seem to take much part in it—at least they don't say or do much.

And then I considered what kind of learning was going on:

This seems like a foreign language class in that much of it involves learning the names of things, learning the vocabulary of physical geology. There isn't much room for discussion of what something is called. Challenging the definition of "mafic" would be as difficult for a student at this level as would challenging the meaning of "sibling" for a beginning ESL student.

Developing Hypotheses My journal entry of June 17, when about one-third of the course had elapsed, shows a first attempt to account in a systematic way for the material I had collected thus far. Using a framework for interpreting journal entries suggested by a study of writing in a philosophy class (North, 1986a), I considered, first, how the "Spaceship Earth" journals could be understood "as rhetorical, part of a transaction with the teacher." I began by speculating that although the entries were not read by their teacher, for my informants they "become an exchange with me, a surrogate for the teacher." Here I seemed to be puzzling out the idea that these entries served some sort of communicative purpose. The problem was that although they looked like conversation—associative, switching topics, referring to their intended reader, and assuming a shared context—they weren't being responded to, at least not by Weber.

I had a clearer idea of the extent to which the journals could be read as disciplinary writing (North, 1986a). I wrote that "[the students] are learning and using a language. The journal is an occasion for practicing that language, to some extent. But insofar as the only geology reading they are required to do is read the textbook, there are no models for what 'geology writing' is, and the course is not [geared to teaching it]." I went on to write that

This is not a course for people who want to be prepared to "write geology." It is, as a gen. ed. class, for dilettantes of the subject. People who need only a familiarity with the language. A class for tourists rather than people intending to live and work in a place. We see the highlights, the symbols, the things that dramatize what's possible.

By that, I meant that because preparation for disciplinary specialization was not an aim of this course, the journals were not assigned to help students think or write like geologists so much as like informed, or at least interested, citizens in a society in which personal and social interests and environmental issues are interconnected.

"As an occasion for intellectual growth," the journals, I thought, also reflected the general education thrust of the course: namely, that the course intended not to specialize its students with technical or methodological information about the science of geology, but to develop or provide support for values that, it seemed to me, my informants had already learned:

> A broadening of perspective is inevitable. And this is a purpose of the course: to teach the interactions of man with his/her environment. But the students I'm following have already come to understand man's potential to influence (devastate) the physical world. They've learned from the news of nuclear accidents and acid rain, from direct and personal experiences of waste disposal leaks . . . that we are endangering our resources.

I went on to write that "This is not like learning Marxism or aesthetics. This course has more to do with providing support for values and illustration of their relevance."

I had decided, then, about half-way through the course, that reading the writing as evidence of intellectual or ethical growth, or as a reflection of the writers' stances vis à vis the community of professional geologists, was less useful as a hypothesis than was understanding it in some way as part of an exchange among members of this particular community. My subsequent procedures were influenced by my interest in understanding how this "exchange" might work: I continued tape-recording and copying what was put on the blackboard, but I also noted anything Weber said or implied to the class about their journals, and took note of any evidence that my informants had Weber—or me—in mind as they were writing. Although it seemed at the time that I was taking my cues about what to ask simply from my informants' interests, transcripts of our interview meetings show that I wanted to know whatever they could tell me about their perception of Weber's expectations of their writing, their speculation about what I later interpreted as the kinds of roles they were taking in responding orally and in writing to him, and the kinds of roles he was taking in responding to them in class.

My June 17 question about the extent to which this class could be read as a community shaped my understanding of the function of journals in "Spaceship Earth." I wanted, in other words, to understand writing as part of what created the "text" of this class: to develop a reading that would interpret the writing in light of "the language in class, behavior . . . conversation outside class and with me." I lacked confidence, though, in a way of doing this, because it didn't seem that, in the field of composition, there was a precedent for what I was dimly aware that I could do with my material.

Where, then, was the key that would unlock the kind of connection I wanted to make? Shortly after the class ended and as I was proposing my research as a dissertation—but before I had begun reading all the journals submitted at the end of class in conjunction with listening to my tapes of class meetings—I came across ideas for describing writing as a communicative process and for describing interconnections among diverse texts that I considered as ways of organizing and focusing my reading of the journals in "Spaceship Earth." The first of these insights came from Lucille McCarthy's (1985) treatment of a college student's texts and his instructor's written responses to them as if they were conversations. Using H. P. Grice's theory of cooperativeness in conversation (Grice, 1975), McCarthy claimed that the student–teacher written interaction was regulated by the extent to which each of them relied on any of four *discourse maxims*: quality, quantity, relation, and manner. Essentially, the extent to which the student and his instructor shared an understanding of what constituted truthfulness (quality), of how much or how little to say (quantity), of what was relevant to the goals of the assignment (relation), and of the appropriate form in writing (manner) was the extent to which their written conversation was successful. Despite my reservations about the extent to which the journal entries could be treated as a dialogue, I thought that analysis of writers' uses of these maxims could at least show how they were attempting to communicate with their instructor.

A few months later, I discovered another set of terms, *iterability* and *presupposition*, taken by James Porter (1986) from Culler's (1981) discussion of *intertextuality* to refer to the way that written texts make use of each other. These principles I thought could be used "to establish this community's cultural and ideological terrain."

My plan, then, as I proposed it in February of 1987, was to look in my text—journals and class transcripts—for evidence of intertextuality: specifically, for what was iterable—essentially, repeatable, and for what was presupposed, or assumed. I thought that, for example, I could use jokes and humorous comments to show shared attitudes toward language or shared values. Then, using Grice's terms, *quantity, quality, manner,* and *relation,* I could look at the extent to which student writers' interpretation, in their journal entries, of these discourse rules matched the instructor's expectations, communicated in his responses to the entries when the term ended.

However, as I began reliving the class by listening to my tapes of each class meeting day, and reading all the journal entries purportedly written on those days, I was to find that Grice's and Culler's terms obscured my view of what was unique to the material I was studying and fragmented the kind of focus I wanted to develop. Reading my texts to find evidence for these maxims seemed to be at odds with my otherwise ethnographic methodology. Furthermore, my student and teacher informants were unlike the socially and politically equal communicators in Grice's hypothetical scenario. As Mary Louise Pratt (1977) has pointed out, Grice's maxims assume that communicators in any situation share objectives and negotiate with each other from positions of equal power. However, the power structure of "Spaceship Earth" was hierarchical. Although students were offered ample opportunity to negotiate with Weber, Weber's status as teacher invested him with power to make all decisions pertaining to the conduct of this class, and despite his expressed interest in negotiating with students, the unevenness of power inherent in their role relationship curtailed negotiation As I listened to the inter view and class transcripts, it seemed to me that my informants' understanding of what was truthful, relevant, and appropriate to say in their journals was shaped by their perception of what Weber—and I—assumed to be truthful, relevant, and appropriate: one's success as a student in this class depended on one's success in approximating our viewpoints.

Furthermore, as it became clearer to me that I wanted to describe how journal keeping assisted the development of the sociopolitical hierarchy in this class, I realized that Culler's terms, derived from analysis of written texts and used to classify connections among written texts, would not serve my purposes as well as terms used to describe social relationships. I was to find that the concept of *role* as articulated by sociologist of education

David Hargreaves (1972) best suited my understanding of what discourse in this classroom—oral, written, and nonverbal—expressed and represented.

Although I set aside the terminology of Grice and of Culler as I began rereading the journals, entries in a second notebook that I used to reflect on the journal texts and class dynamics show my interest in finding connections among the journals and relationships between the journal entries and activities in class. My list of what the journals had in common was very much like my transcript of what Weber had said the journals were to be used for. But my early hypothesis that students were simply "following through on what [Weber] had essentially told them to do" was challenged by my discovery, in listening to the class tapes, that Weber's repeated requests for students to ask questions and bring up topics of their own choosing in class were not being followed through. Thus I hypothesized that this class was "silent partly because they can respond to [CW] in the journals—contrary to evidence that writing/freewriting, etc. in classes increases the amount of student participation, here it seems to have the opposite effect." I needed to revise this hypothesis when I found a question asked in a journal was raised in class the next day: "When [CW] asked for questions (as he had when this journal question was asked), then journal entries could serve as material for students to ask about." Then, when I listened in the class tapes to what happened when students asked questions (in the first week, only twice) that were raised in their journals, I heard Weber elaborating on points he had lectured about the day the entries were written. Thus I hypothesized that "when asked in class, questions raised in the journals encourage lecturing."

The first set of possible connections I considered between journal keeping and what happened in class were topical and formal. How much of the lecture material was recounted in the entries? When Weber suggested using *Science News* articles as sources for information, how many entries made reference to these articles? Then I began to consider the relevance of journal keeping to the structure of the class agenda. I was particularly interested in any references in the journals to class activities—to complaints about tests, for example, or to difficulties with lecture or text material. Using the entries and the interview and class transcripts, I made notes of any possible effects journal keeping might have had: first, on what writers said and how Weber responded in class; second, on what was written on the board or otherwise publicly demonstrated; third, on how students were tested, and how knowledge was defined and organized in this class; and fourth, on how relationships among my informants, their instructor and their journal reader(s) developed.

As I began to identify connections among class activities and journal keeping, I sensed that these connections were subtle and often inexplicit. Why was the journal not used more explicitly and more often in this class? How had it happened that Weber, an outspoken advocate of writing across the curriculum, and Beth, Tina, Jill, and Jim, who were interested students and active, academically successful writers, all made such limited use of these journals? Why did it seem that Weber's stated goals for journal keeping were at odds with the ways his students were using their journals? My conversations with Weber about his professional history and the history and curricular role of the course suggested that my account of journal keeping would need to extend beyond class activities.

As I was considering and abandoning various ways of classifying my material, I was increasingly to focus on these questions: How were the journal entries helping writers with what they were doing in class? How were the journal entries reflecting what they had told me about their interests and experiences? How did the assignment fit in with what I had learned about the teacher who used it and the history of the course he used it in? Deciding that the students' and their teacher's uses for journals could not neatly be classified as social, political, or curricular, but rather some combination of all three, I arrived, at last, at the interpretation of journal keeping that I detail in the next three chapters.

3

JOURNAL KEEPING
AND CLASS ACTIVITY
IN "SPACESHIP EARTH"

This chapter explores the interrelation of journal keeping and classroom activity in Earth Science 87:036, "Spaceship Earth." Classroom activity included assignment making, lecturing, in-class writing, discussion, and testing. Although the dominant and focal activity of the class was Professor Weber's lecturing, students participated by asking and answering questions, presenting their opinions of nuclear energy development in a debate, writing in their journals about the significance of the light bulb, and taking three multiple-choice exams. Journal texts, class transcripts, and students' conversations with me suggest three ways journals were used in or in connection with class activity. Students used their journals to *interact* with their instructor and with each other, to *prepare* for tests, and to *respond* to the information presented them and the way it was presented in class. These categories overlap; many entries that respond to class activities (typically by praising or critiquing them) also helped their authors prepare for upcoming events; some of these entries were then used in exchanges between writer and instructor. Furthermore, whether students wrote journal entries to review Weber's lectures, help them study, or remind them of questions to ask Weber, they all did so in response to what they thought Weber would accept from them. Thus I introduce my discussion of functions of journal keeping by describing how Weber made the assignment and how his students' journals reflect the expectations he communicated.

The Journal Assignment: Responding to Weber's Expectations

The journal assignment in "Spaceship Earth" was not a single or fixed directive. Students' journals responded to expectations that their instructor communicated explicitly when he made the assignment on the first day of class and implicitly when he referred to journals at various times during the semester. Journal entries were influenced not only by Professor Weber's directions for this assignment, but also by the kind of persona Weber projected when he introduced the course and its requirements. When Weber described the assignment and illustrated it with entries written for an earlier class, some of the expectations made explicit in his printed instructions were reinforced; others were minimized. Expectations of journal writing communicated during the first class meeting were modified in later references to and uses of journals in class.

Defining the Assignment: Explicit Expectations Weber introduced the journal assignment as he explained course requirements on the first day of class, June 9, 1986. Figure 7 reproduces the syllabus he distributed. After identifying the purposes of "Spaceship Earth" (a general eduction course intending "to show the interaction between geological materials, processes and . . . our society") Weber described class procedures and conduct. He told students that he expected them to attend the "two hours per day of lecture, five days a week," but the atmosphere would be informal. "I tell crummy jokes," he said, "[but] I will continue telling them. If you think there may have been a joke, go ahead and laugh . . . if you get too dull, I'm going to make you do exercises." Then Weber described course requirements in earnest. After telling students they could expect three multiple-choice exams and, possibly, unannounced quizzes, Weber introduced the journal: "Another requirement of this course [which] is ungraded but you will have to do it to earn the grade you get is a journal."

After commenting briefly on the textbook and explaining his test grading procedures, Weber returned to the journal assignment. A printed handout distributed to the class (Figure 8) served as the basis for his explanation of what he expected.

This handout, "Spaceship Earth Journal Assignment," outlines several expectations of journal keeping that Weber and 16 of the 17 students enrolled in his course regarded as nonnegotiable. All of the students who completed the course (one took an incomplete) adhered to the procedural requirements that introduce the first four paragraphs of this document. They all handed in their journals at the end of the course, made the entries in a bound notebook, and dated each entry. Although most students did not write one entry each day for each of the 19 days of class, all made it appear they had done so.

All but one of the students who completed the course also adhered to Weber's requirement that the journal not be a "diary." Weber put in writing and told his class: "I do not want a diary! Who you had dinner with last night, what your mother thought about your new dress . . . is not suitable material." Two students, Carole and Kay, acknowledged this requirement explicitly in their journals. After the first test, both referred to but did not elaborate on personal difficulties because, as Kay wrote, "I know this isn't a diary, so I won't go into it." Carole also mentioned, but did not detail "certain pressures" that contributed to her difficulty with the first test.

After telling students what the entries shouldn't be, Weber, following his handout, suggested sources for entries: "Entries you make which are not assigned in class can be suggested by reading you do or experiences you have." The suggestion that entries address "reading you do [of] . . . newsworthy geological events in the papers, magazines, on radio and TV" influenced nine of the 18 journals. Of these, only two made more than occasional reference to local news items of geological interest. In 15 of his 19 entries, Jim reported briefly on geological current events he had read or heard about on a televised news program, *Time* magazine, or the local daily newspaper; Tina, a physics major with a subscription to *Science News,* summarized short features on the physics of volcanos and earthquakes in 13 of her 20 entries.

Weber also advised students to use personal experiences relevant to geological issues as sources for entries. Six students occasionally referred to their experiences with geological materials (rock collecting), hazards (flooding or toxic farm chemicals), and processes (what they learned in high school about continental drift, earthquakes, or volcano formation). Connections between personal experience and geological topics were typically unelaborated. Roger's entry of June 19, for example, anticipates a connection: "It would be interesting to return to some of my previous

FIGURE 7   "Spaceship Earth" Syllabus, Distributed June 9

SYLLABUS
SPACESHIP EARTH 87:036
Summer, 1986

Dr.
Room 166 Baker   273-   , 277-

Welcome to Spaceship Earth. This syllabus is intended to provide
you with an overview of the course and to answer some of your
initial questions, such as: "What is expected of me in this
course?" "How will my grade in this course be determined?

Spaceship Earth is a geology course which emphasizes the
interaction of humans with the earth. Life and human culture
evolved and presently exists on this planet as a result of
organisms and communities taking advantage of or being able to
tolerate geologic materials (minerals, rocks, air, water, soil)
and changes in the configurations of these materials brought
about by geologic processes (volcanism, erosion, flooding,
etc.). Everything we do involves these interactions. We have
generally managed pretty well, but sometimes we run into
problems when we ignore or misunderstand geologic conditions. It
is the objective of this course to build an understanding and
appreciation of geology and how it relates to our lives.

The class will meet five times each week. You are expected to
come to class. If you miss a lecture, you are still responsible
for the material covered, and for the exams. You cannot do well
in this course if you do not attend class.

The grade you receive in this course will be based upon the
percentage of correct answers to three multiple-choice
examinations of about 50 questions each plus several unannounced
quizzes.

The required text for this course is Environmental Geology by
Carla Montgomery, W.C. Brown, publisher, 1986.

Spaceship Earth is a general education course designed for
persons who have not taken other geology courses. If you have
had physical geology, either her at UNI or elsewhere, you should
consider dropping the course.

I prefer to keep the atmosphere in the class informal. You
should feel comfortable in asking questions and volunteering
your ideas in discussion. Since we will be covering a lot of
material that will, presumably, be new to you, lots of questions
should arise in the progression of the lectures. If I don't
answer them, you should ask for clarification. Do not sit there

FIGURE 7 (CONT.)   "Spaceship Earth" Syllabus, Distributed June 9

silently drowning in a sea of unasked questions!!! If you have a question, chances are great that others in the room have the same question.

Normally, I do not post office hours but I do have an open door. Anytime you want to discuss anything with me, give me a call, or we can set up an appointment after class. If you find me in my office or lab (Room 8 Physics) I'll generally be able to talk with you. You have my office and home phone numbers on this syllabus. Part of my job is to help you in matters related to the course or any aspect of your life here at the University, but you must initiate the contact if you have a concern and want to talk about it.

KEEP THIS SYLLABUS FOR FUTURE REFERENCE!!!!

TENTATIVE SCHEDULE OF TOPICS

SPACESHIP EARTH
Summer 1986

DATE	TOPIC	TEXT CHAPTER
M	Intro. to course, geology, space and time	
T	Big Bang, the universe, the solar system	1
W	Major features of the earth, plate tectonics	4
Th	Minerals, rocks, rock cycle	3
F	Sedimentary rocks, geologic time, EXAMINATION	Appendix A
M	Nature of geologic hazards, volcanic hazards	6
T	Earthquakes	5
W	Mass movement	9
Th	Underground hazards, flooding	7
F	Flooding, coastal hazards, EXAMINATION	10
M	Significance of the lightbulb, resources	2, Sec. XX
T	Water resources, soil	12, 13
W	Mineral resources	14
Th	Energy resources	15, 16
F	Pollution and waste disposal	17, 18, 19
M	Waste disposal	21
T	Class debate on nuclear energy or other topic	
W	Climatic change, nuclear winter	
Th	Celebration of the earth, FINAL EXAMINATION	

FIGURE 8   Description of Journal Assignment
Distributed to Spaceship Earth Students June 9, 1986

SPACESHIP EARTH JOURNAL ASSIGNMENT

Summer 1986

One of the requirements of this course is the keeping of a
personal journal to be handed in at the end of the course. No
grade will be given to this journal, but it must adhere to the
assignment to be accepted. An unacceptable journal (or no
journal at all) will cost you one full letter grade for the
course.

The journal must be a bound notebook (no looseleaf bundles or
pads of note paper) dedicated to this one purpose: that is, do
not use a notebook that you use for other purposes. A fifty-page
5 x 7 spiralbound book is quite acceptable, but if you enjoy
writing in larger books, that would be fine also. Do not waste
your money on one that is too big.

You shall make five entries each week from the first day of
class to the last. Some of these entries will be made (or
started) in class. Whether initiated in class or by you, the
content of each entry should be your thoughtful reflections on
the topic. I do not want a diary! Who you had dinner with last
night, what your mother thought about your new dress, or the
mileage you get in your car, now that you changed the plugs, is
not suitable material for this journal. On the other hand, the
entries need not be strictly geological, but they should have
some relevance to the course. Some of the entries will be
assigned topics--which means that you should bring your journals
to class each and every time. We will also discuss what persons
have written. Entries you make which are not assigned can be
suggested by reading you do or experiences you have. Part of the
purpose of the journal is to make you aware of things going on
in the world that have some connection with what we are studying
in this course. From now to the end of the semester, there will
be earthquakes, volcanoes, floods, and other newsworthy
geological events in the papers, magazines, and on radio and TV.
There will also be plenty of environmental topics covered as
well. A good place to get inspirations for your journal is the
periodicals section of the library. If you haven't been there,
GO!!!

Each entry must be dated--the date you actually do the writing.
Do not save up your writing and then put down many entries in a
short time--that is not acceptable. The journal need not be
written in a formal style. Regard it as thinking on paper. You
are writing for yourself, not me, and the only way you will be
penalized is if you don't write. Spelling, punctuation, etc. for
this journal are not important. From time to time throughout the
semester I may ask to see your journal to see how you are doing.

The journal is yours and as long as you meet the requirements
set forth here, it will be acceptable for this course. It should
be a recording of your thinking--and if you are not thinking,
you really ought to get into the practice!!!!

vacation spots and be able to apply knowledge of rock formation and to meditate on how the landscape had evolved to its present day appearance." Three students—Beth, Darryl, and Roger—sustained reference to their own experience in any one entry for more than three sentences, and they addressed their experiences outside of this class in more than five entries.

In addition to indicating acceptable topics, the journal assignment handout also characterizes the anticipated rhetoric of entries as "thoughtful reflections on the topic." It indicates that journal writing, in part, should make connections among "things going on in the world" and "what we are studying in this course." Several students—Beth, Roger, Darryl, and Jim—connected their own experiences of geological processes and hazards, or Weber's presentations on these subjects, with larger sociopolitical issues. Jim, for example, referred to the role water rights play in the federal government's treatment of Native Americans, Roger and Jim speculated about reasons people are attracted to geological hazards, and Darryl considered the sociopolitical ramifications of mineral distribution. Of the four students whose entries addressed the connections that Weber's handout advises writers to "reflect" on, two, Darryl and Roger, sustained attention to a single topic throughout a given entry.

Illustrating the Assignment: Implicit Expectations Weber's handout and description of the journal assignment were not the only information his students received about journals on the first day of class. As he explained the assignment, Weber held up two spiral bound notebooks, journals submitted in an earlier class. Then he used an overhead projector to illustrate what they contained. Some of these transparencies are reproduced as Figure 9. He read aloud from each projected entry, characterizing it ("this one is a reaction to the lecture"), interpreting what he read ("she's thinking," and "that's an expression of feeling"), and suggesting topics ("this one concerns the religious significance of what I've been talking about").

Because all of the sample entries commented on "Spaceship Earth" class activities—six of the seven addressed Weber's lectures—students in the summer 1986 class assumed it would be acceptable for them to do likewise. The first of the sample entries, titled "Thoughts about: Lecture notes about the crust," raised a question about Weber's information, as did the second, titled "Plate Tectonics." The third, "Lecture topic: Gross Structure of the Universe," fourth, "After the Test," and fifth (untitled)

FIGURE 9 Journal Entry Samples Projected for Class, June 9th

2:00 P.M.   Mon. Jan. 28, 1985

Thoughts about:
Lecture notes about the crust. 4/9

I know that I take a lot of the "facts"
you give us for granted, but the ocean
crust being younger then the continental crust just doesn't make sense.
If the crust was made evenly then
it would ✗ have uniform thickness
and age then when the water
came from the atmosphere and
settled then the weight made
the pliable mantle move aside so
the crust would dip and oceans
would settle deeper and deeper
into the center of the earth or
over flow onto the continents.
The crust is what it is and
can't be older or younger than
itself.

FIGURE 9 (CONT.) Journal Entry Samples Projected for Class, June 9th

6:00 p.m.   Wed. 1-30-85

~~Platitectonics~~
Plate Tectonics

Boy, am I glad you didn't see my
hand go up before you started the lecture.
I would have questioned you about the
crust age. I even read the Volcanism
chapter in the text. I guess I
missed the part of new crust being
created.

I don't understand why the specific
plates movements doesn't have some pattern to
them. It would seem neat and orderly
if the plates moved with or against
the magnetic flow or something.
Luck for us this phenomenon
is slow.

What makes ~~this~~ the plates keep
moving in a specific, continuous
movement? If this continues
for however long,

FIGURE 9 (CONT.)   Journal Entry Samples Projected for Class, June 9th

12:25 p.m.   AFTER THE TEST   2-22-85

Well it has been a while since my last
entry but I've been studying. I hope I
did well. Since the test is over I don't
dwell on it but go onto new material. Well
not quite. In my limited ability I want
to put down on paper what I was
toying with:

The idea of the expanding universe.

Suppose our universe was as dynamic
as our earth. The big bang being
somewhere-anywhere, say here.
And us (our universe here)

While our universe is expanding other
debri could be getting caught up into the ex-
pansion. Sometimes providing enough matter to
continue to expand further. But!! If there
isn't enough matter then the process collapses
in leaving out solar systems in equalibrium or
able to be drawn into another universe.

FIGURE 9 (CONT.) Journal Entry Samples Projected for Class, June 9th

Will the continents ever join again? What creates new lithosphere? I know where - at the oceanic ridge, but why? What could cause this on-going process? I am intrigued at the idea of a continuously changing/renewing earth.

Since the continental crust elements, rocks, formation, or whatever is different then the oceanic crust, is it constantly changing and renewing itself also?

I'm also glad you point out things that science can't explain yet, like the volcanoes that occur inland.

raised questions about Weber's discussion of cosmology. After seeing these sample entries, ten of 16 students whose first entries were dated June 9 reported on the first day's class. They used similar language in establishing this class as their context, writing, for example, "Today was the first day of class," "Today was the first meeting," "Well, the first day is over and it wasn't too bad," or "Today is the first day of class in Spaceship Earth and we are going to have our first test on Friday." Most students continued to address class activities in their journal entries, responding to Weber's material or his methods of presenting it in ways I detail later in this chapter.

The sample entries are also a part of what accounts for the rhetoric of journal entries submitted to Weber in the summer of 1986. Weber had characterized journal entries as "thoughtful reflections." Nonetheless, all of the sample entries expressed what appeared to be spontaneous feelings of interest, curiosity, amazement, confusion, or frustration. All of these but frustration are the sentiments expressed in the June 9, 1986, entries, in which writers declare their interest in the course and their awe, confusion, or curiosity about the cosmological topics Weber discussed. From the sample entries, students also learned that complaints were acceptable; Weber read aloud from an entry that began, "The first test in this class. Boy it makes me mad/frustrated. I studied hard and didn't get a chance to show what I really meant." Weber commented on this entry, saying, "Well, that's an expression of feeling, an emotional response. Sometimes people get really nasty but later on nice so it balances out." Here, his students received a mixed message. Weber demonstrated that he accepted "nastiness," but he also implied that entries "balanced out" criticism in the long run. Like the entry he projected, many entries written later in the '86 class described their authors' frustration about the tests. Yet, as in the samples, criticism of tests and other assigned activities was "balanced" by praise, typically for Weber's teaching methods.

Furthermore, although Weber told his students and put in writing that students were to write for themselves and not for him in their journals, half of the sample entries addressed him in the second person; in the summer '86 journals, six of 15 entries dated June 9 address Weber in the second or third person. Although most writers made Weber their audience as they praised him (as does the sample writer who is "glad you point out things science can't explain yet"), a few students addressed Weber in the second person when they critiqued his material. The author of the first sample began an entry, "I know that I take a lot of the facts you give us for granted, but the ocean crust being younger then the continental crust just doesn't make sense." Howard, a summer '86 student, similarly addressed Weber as he challenged Weber's information on June 9: "Today you compared the science involved in determining [cosmological theory] with that of medicine, I do not see any connection."

Weber's illustration of the journal assignment influenced the format as well as the topics and rhetoric of his students' entries. Although the printed directions did not require that the journal be a spiral bound notebook, Weber's holding up two such notebooks lessened the possibility any student would choose, say, a three-ring binder or a report folder to submit the journal in. (All of the 1986 "Spaceship Earth" journals were spiral-bound notebooks.) Furthermore, though Weber had not indicated he expected titles or entry headings, four of the six entries Weber projected for the class were, as I've indicated, headed with titles that referred to a class topic. Six of 16 summer '86 students titled their first entries, Tina with "Lecture on Gross Structure of the Universe," Sue with "Lecture: Distance and Time," Karen with "Introduction to Course, Geology, Space and Time," Darryl with "Intro to Course," Beth with "Spaceship Earth Journal," and John K. with "Journal." Sue, Darryl, and Karen continued to title their entries, Sue and Karen with reference to the topics planned (i.e., listed on the syllabus) for the class days their entries were dated, Darryl with reference to topics that were actually addressed.

Introducing the Course: Implicit Expectations of Journal Keeping   Further explanation for the rhetoric of journal entries can be found in the way Weber introduced and set the tone for this course. Students were encouraged to communicate with Weber in their entries, not only because the sample entries did so and because Weber's directions indicated he would read the journals, but also because Weber impressed the class with his affability and approachability. (When I asked Beth how she would explain the journal assignment to a student who had missed the first class, she said, "I would explain it by explaining [Weber].") Weber told students in his syllabus, "I have an open door. Part of my job is to help you in matters related to the course or any aspect of your life." He joked with the class (about the name of the course) and teased them (for not recognizing that he punned on the word "granite" as he read a sample entry). The friendly interest he took in his students and his repeated requests for questions or comments suggested he wanted them to communicate with him.

If Weber's persona helps to explain his students' attempts to communicate with him in their first entries and their expressions of interest in his material and manner, the inherently dramatic subjects of his June 9 lecture—the immensity of space and the infinity of time—could also be expected to provoke interest. But an equally compelling explanation for the number of entries that summarized or otherwise recounted not only this, but many of Weber's subsequent lectures, can be found in his description of the way students would be evaluated in this class. Weber explained that students' grades would be determined primarily by their scores on three multiple-choice exams, the first of which was Friday, June 13, the last day of the first week of class. He was neither asked for nor did he offer advice to students about how they might profitably prepare for this test. Assuming that doing well on Weber's tests would count for more in their final grade than meeting his expectations of their journals, several students ignored his suggestions they write about geological current events, their personal experiences of course topics, or connections among them. Instead, they used their journals as study guides in the ways described later in this chapter.

Redefining the Assignment The expectations Weber communicated to students on the first day of class were the first of several interactions pertaining to journal keeping that influenced students' ideas of what they should be writing about in their journals. On June 16 and June 20, Weber asked students if they had any questions about the journal keeping, prompting exchanges that affected his students' perceptions of what he expected, and their subsequent entries. On July 2, he suggested that students use their final entries to evaluate the course, prompting many to do so.

A week from the Monday he made the assignment, during an exchange with students at the beginning of class about scheduling the second test, Weber asked if there were "any questions or comments on the journals." When Kay asked about procedure—"you said [you wanted entries] every day. You meant Sunday through Friday or?"—Weber responded that it didn't matter which days students made entries so long as they wrote five times a week. Weber's response is part of what prompted as many as half his students to make it appear they had written five entries each week, each on a different day of the week. Most students, especially during the last two weeks of the course, fell behind the schedule Weber indicated he expected. Jill, for example, told me that she hadn't made any entries between June 20 and 24. On the 24th, when Weber asked students to write in their journals in class, Jill left ten pages blank between her June 19th entry and the in-class writing she started. Then, when she decided to get caught up on the 25th, she began filling in the blank pages with entries for the 20th and 23rd. She tore out blank pages remaining between the entries dated 6/23 and 6/24.

On June 16, after Weber responded to Kay's question about journal writing logistics, Jim (the only student who consistently used entries to comment on geological current events), asked whether "reading material" should be referenced. Weber responded, "If you're commenting about or responding to some article you've read, put in the name . . . but don't give me a lot of references . . . in the journal." On June 20, after reporting on a *Science* article questioning the Big Bang theory, Weber said that "if you're looking for sources for your journal, then *Science* magazine is one of those places you might go." Tina then offered another source: "*Science News* is good," she said.

Jim's question on the 16th about citing sources, together with Weber's and Tina's comments on the 20th, suggested to at least two students that, in writing as they had about Weber's lecture topics or about their own experience with geological hazards, they weren't meeting his expectations. Beth and Howard responded with surprise in their journals to what they took to be an indication that they were expected to consult "articles of research," as Beth put it: "My journal is not over articles of research," reads her entry for June 23, "because I understood the instruction sheet to instruct us to write as though we were thinking to ourselves so that's what I'm going to do." In an entry dated June 20, Howard wrote that "I just found out today that I have been doing this wrong. I didn't know we were supposed to be looking up articles. No wonder I've been having trouble coming up with things to write." Although Weber's comments on the 20th had not explicitly directed students to use sources ("if you need sources . . . " he had said), they were heard as directive. Many more entries addressed newspaper or magazine articles after this class period than were written about news articles before it. (Beth, for example, after declaring in the entry cited above that she would continue to use her own experience in the journal, went on to comment on a campus newspaper report on unpredicted subsidence under a science building.)

Some students were influenced by what Weber, with Tina's and Jeff's help, suggested he expected of entry sources. However, only three students, Dixie, Jim, and Tina, exclusively addressed any entries to outside reading. Students referred to what they had heard about current events, as did John K., for example, when he wrote, "heard about the Indonesian earthquakes." But these references typically follow commentary (described later in this chapter) on material Weber presented. References to personal experience—the other part of Weber's explicit assignment—are somewhat more widely represented in the journals than are geological current events. But like the brief reports of current events, references to personal experience are typically subordinated to description of class activities.

One reason that fewer than a third of the entries reflect what Weber asked for in his handout is that the written directions were not significantly reinforced in his subsequent references to or use of the journals. Weber later told me (as he had noted on the assignment sheet) that he wanted this assignment to prompt students to use the library. Because he chose not to read the journals when class was in session, however, he did not see that students were making little use of periodical sources. Beth and Howard heard as a direction Weber's suggestion on June 20 that they use such sources. But after a brief flurry of reference to current events, most writers resumed commenting on class, asking questions for more information or otherwise responding to Weber's material. For the most part, they used their journals not to respond to outside sources but, instead, to interact with and respond to their instructor, and to prepare for activities in which they were required to participate.

Classroom Functions of Journal Keeping

Promoting Verbal Interaction Encouraged by the sample entries to communicate with Weber in their journals, and encouraged by Weber to ask him questions, several students raised questions in their journals that they later asked in class. They used journals in other kinds of interaction as well. Half of the students who participated in the class discussion of nuclear energy (organized as a debate) chose to use their journals in preparing for or presenting their arguments to each other. A week before the nuclear energy debate, Weber made the journal a prelude to discussion by asking students to share their responses to an in-class journal writing exercise.

Student-Initiated Interaction: Asking Questions At least twice during the course, Beth asked Weber questions she had raised in her journal. Karen raised a question in her journal that her mother and fellow student, Carole, asked in class; Carole also raised questions in her journal which prompted her to ask Weber to clarify his expectations of the final exam.

In her first entry, Beth wrote that "we have barely scratched the surface of the information available in this class and already I have a million questions forming in my mind." She used several entries to remind her to ask Weber what she wanted to know. In an entry written at the end of the first week of class, she wrote: "I am going to ask about petrified wood before the four weeks is over if he doesn't mention it on his own. He will probably tell me it's scared. Ha ha." Ten class days later, Beth asked Weber about the composition of pearls. When Weber, in answering her, referred to the way wood deteriorates, she asked, "You said one time about everything deteriorating. What makes petrified wood?"

After Weber's first lecture, on space and time, Beth wrote that "imagin[ing] an infinite universe staggers my mind." When Weber asked for questions about the Big Bang during the next hour of class, Beth's response reflected her difficulty grasping that the universe is infinite:

Beth: But . . . can you comprehend that there's no end at all?

Weber: The astronomers say, no, that there is an end to space. Space itself . . . is the limits of the Big Bang. But . . . I can't visualize that. . . . [I have] private reservations about the Big Bang. . . .

Beth's questions here prompted Weber to elaborate, not only on the prospect of new cosmological theory, but on the way scientific discoveries are driven by new methodologies that "revise our picture of the universe."

As Weber provided evidence for the Big Bang, he sketched a galaxy on the blackboard. Talking about the origin of our solar system, Weber pointed to one of the spiraling arms radiating from the core of his galaxy drawing. Weber's use of his drawing confused Karen, who thought that only the arm he pointed to contained a solar system. Karen wrote in her journal after class that "If our solar system is located on one arm of the galaxy why isn't there other solar systems on the other arms or how did all of the planets land on this one arm?" Karen continued, "When I asked my mom the questions, she came up with more." When Weber began the next day's class by asking if there were any questions about the Big Bang, he acknowledged Karen's mother, Carole, who asked, "When you were showing us the galaxy yesterday and you showed us one of the arms, you said that the solar system formed on one of those arms. Why aren't there solar systems on the rest of the arms?"

Like Beth's question about infinity and space, Carole's question prompted Weber to clarify and elaborate, redrawing the galaxy and using an analogy to suggest the extent to which intergalactic space may be populated with stars. As Weber sketched the radiating arms of a galaxy on the board, he said

> There very well could be . . . a million solar systems out there . . . the spiral arms coming out . . . sorta look like [this]. Now how many stars are in there? If you look at the pieces of chalk . . . with a microscope you would see . . . really a whole bunch of wee little tiny specks of chalk . . . you could imagine each one of those . . . specks of chalk in that mark as being stars . . . several light years from every other star. . . . We may not be so unique. On the other hand, we might be. . . .

Weber went on to speculate on the possibilities of life elsewhere for several minutes before introducing his planned topic (dynamic systems).

In the foregoing interactions, journal entries prompted questions which, in turn, prompted Weber to review and elaborate on earlier topics before introducing new ones. The students' part in these interactions was brief: despite Weber's expressed willingness to "go off on tangents," students did not typically follow up their requests for information. Beth speculated they were reluctant to lead Weber away from material he would hold them responsible for on tests. Beth was probably right; her classmates did follow up their questions about Weber's plans for exams. At least one line of questioning about test material can be traced to a journal entry.

In this case, Carole raised questions in her journal that antic-ipated her questions in class about the final exam. Her 6/25 journal entry reports that

Today's lecture on mineral resources was somewhat inter-esting, but I think several of the categories along with their subcategories will only cause confusion in my trying to remember if a mineral is a metal or a non-metal? . . . If a mineral is a construction or a chemical material? or what are the most common uses? and where are they mined? . . . It seems as if I'm headed for mass confusion on the final exam.

Confusion here names Carole's uncertainty about how much of Weber's information about minerals—supplemented in the text-book with detailed production and distribution charts—she would need to memorize for the final. In class the next day, June 26, Carole asked Weber how he would test the class on mineral consumption and production.

Carole: In studying from the textbook, we're getting a lot of . . . worldwide and . . . U.S. statistics. Should we focus on one more than the other?

Weber: Well . . . the kinds of statistics that appear on the charts and tables and so on . . . normally I stay away from . . . what I want you to do . . . is get a feel for the magnitude of those numbers. . . . I might ask you about the world's supply of molybdenum but it doesn't matter very much . . . that you know that the U.S. has something like 60 percent . . . of the world's reserves. What you ought to know is . . . we've got a lot of molybdenum and we don't have much nickel and tin and chromium. That's the . . . significant part.

Carole pressed Weber for a more specific answer:

Well see now what you're talking about is U.S. resources and consumption. That's my point. Should we focus more on U.S.?

Weber answered yes and went on to say, "you [should] know some-thing about U.S. consumption and patterns and supplies" but "you can't be expected to learn in four weeks of 'Spaceship Earth' everything we've covered here, including world supply and U.S. supply and consumption rates, and so on, of a dozen different mineral commodities." Not satisfied, Carole asked again about the statistical information on supply and consumption rates:

Carole: What about the material in the boxes?

Weber: Oh, that's good stuff.

Carole: I know it's good but is it test material?

Weber: It's good stuff. It could be test material, yeah . . . .

Although Weber answered Carole ambiguously here ("material in the boxes"—statistical information—was what he had just said he wouldn't hold students responsible for), Carole's and others' questions about the final exam gave Weber reason to distribute a final exam review sheet the following Monday (June 30). (Weber told me he "[had] the idea students need this sort of thing.") Ten minutes of class time on July 2 was given to discussion of the review sheet: Weber asked students to "scratch off" terms that wouldn't be on the exam because, he said, "we didn't get to them"; he explained several terms that "would be on the test." Explanation of one of the items on the sheet (*Albedo*) structured his introduction to the day's subject of climatic change. In this case, then, a journal entry is one of the reasons, not only for an exchange between Carole and Weber, but also for a change in Weber's plans for the class (his decision to use a review sheet) and in the resulting agenda for discussion.

Student-Initiated Interaction: Debating Nuclear Energy Development   In the isolated instances I've described, three students asked Weber questions they raised in their journals. A larger number—eight—used their journals in preparing for a class participation activity organized as a debate on the pros and cons of nuclear energy. On June 26, a Thursday, Weber divided the class into two groups. As members of the board of a hypothetical power company, the "pro" group was assigned to argue for building a nuclear-fired power plant, the "con" group against it. The following Tuesday, after meeting separately for 15 minutes, the groups reconvened for the debate. Weber called on the pronuclear group to present its arguments first: Scott, Jill, Dixie, Carole, Kay, and Darryl each spoke to the class from the front of the room for about five minutes. Next each member of the antinuclear group—Howard, Karen, Tina, Beth, Sue, Jim, and Gary—presented arguments. Soliciting responses from the reassembled class, Weber then listed on the blackboard nine points made in favor of development of nuclear energy, and nine opposing points. After a ten-minute break, the class reconvened for a "rebuttal" structured by these points: Weber asked, "What's wrong with the point that . . . ," prompting most of the class to redefend or challenge each other's information and opinions.

Although they weren't assigned to do so, three students on the pro side—Scott, Dixie, and Kay—and four on the con side—Beth, Sue, Jim, and Gary—used their journals in preparing for the debate. Dixie, Beth, and Scott used their journals as "a start," in Beth's words—a place to express their opinions, before doing any research. Kay, Sue, and Gary used their journals to report on what they planned to say. Jim made notes in his journal from which he spoke to the class. All seven used their entries to rehearse or structure the arguments they presented and the contributions they made to the rebuttal activity. Since Weber had said he wanted the debaters to be "well-informed" and "enthusiastic," students who used their journals to prepare for the debate also demonstrated to their reader that they were doing their homework, thereby developing rapport with him in their journals, as I will suggest later in this chapter. But first I describe here the role journal keeping played in an activity that was influenced more than any other by students' contributions.

Assigned by Weber to take the con side, Beth wrote in her journal on June 26 that "The electricity purchased by the REC [Rural Electric Cooperative] for my farm is from a nuclear power plant and is quite high in price. On the other hand Independence [a neighboring town] gets theirs from a non-nuclear source for a much cheaper rate. That is a starting point." Although cost to consumers was not a point that Beth chose to make in arguing against nuclear plant construction to a hypothetical audience of fellow power-company board members, she used her journal observation about consumer cost during the rebuttal. In a pause during an exchange between Weber and another student about the costs of nuclear plants, Beth offered that "I get energy from DeWayne Arnold [a nuclear plant]. It's higher than . . . the places where they use coal fired." Weber countered that transmission lines are interconnected; everybody "puts power into the grid and everybody takes it out," he said. Beth persisted: "I don't know, but what I'm going on is the REC told me they buy theirs from DeWayne Arnold . . . at a cost higher than what LaPorte City pays for using [coal fired electricity from another county]." Although Beth's point was contradicted, it was the first of several comments about the costs of nuclear energy which persuaded the group that, from an economic standpoint, nuclear plant construction was doomed.

Beth's entry was, she told me, "the first thing that came into my head about [nuclear energy]." Others' entries written before the debate refer to their authors' research into costs or consequences of nuclear energy. Scott, for example, reports that "After going to the library today for a couple of hours studying for the debate tomorrow I really don't understand why we keep burning coal for energy. It is so dirty and wasteful that I think it is still very dangerous but it is so much . . . cleaner than coal that I think it would be used more" (6/30). Like Beth, he chose not to focus his presentation to the class on the journal subject (one of his team members had "better stats on . . . pollution," he said), but he concluded his argument by saying "The mining of the coal also produces a lot of air pollution, that's not good." To Weber's blackboard list of pronuclear points, Scott contributed, "It's a lot cleaner than coal."

Sue, Gary, and Kay—as did Scott—used entries to report, reflect on, and, in Gary's case, rehearse a persuasive rhetoric. Unlike Scott, these three were able to use most of the material their journals reported on in their talks to the class and in the rebuttal activity. Sue's June 30 entry announces that "tomorrow is our class debate over nuclear power plants. I'm con, and I guess somewhat prepared. My argument is that insurance for the plants itself is quite high, but not nearly enough to cover the damages of a nuclear power plant's failure." Sue elaborated on this point in speaking to the group: "As the nuclear power industry is presently designed, investors in financial institutions refuse to put up the capital, leaving the risk uninsurable. Insurance industries believe the risk of a catastrophic event is too great to insure nuclear power plants at an affordable rate." She detailed the costs: "In 1957, there was an amendment added to the AEC limiting the liabilities of all parties for any nuclear accident up to 560 million dollars. Under the new extension, private insurance will pay 160 million dollars, the nuclear power industry pays 335 million . . . and the taxpayers pay the remaining 165 million." To Weber's list of connuclear points, Sue contributed "Long-term overall cost."

Like Scott, Kay, assigned to the pro side, used a journal entry to express something of what she learned from preparing her opinion. "After much research," she wrote June 30, "I would feel much safer having a nuclear plant near me than I would a coal powered plant. I think the dangers of nuclear plants have many safety devices to control them, whereas I see nothing to stop the sulphur and carbon polluting our air from coal burning." In her presentation to the class, Kay elaborated on the safety features of nuclear reactors: "They constructed a steel vessel around the reactor that is three inches thick, and around that they've put another steel vessel [to contain hot contaminated water], then around the whole reactor system they've made a concrete building that is three feet thick, and it's virtually impossible for any [radioactive] substances to leak out." Kay concluded her presentation with mention of the second argument her journal entry addressed: the pollution generated by coal-fired plants. She cited numbers of people "who die prematurely from air pollution due to the burning of coal, and to the lung cancer and respiratory diseases . . . no solution yet to all the sulphur that's being put into the air from coal." To Weber's pronuclear list, Kay contributed that "[nuclear plants] are safer now than they were in 1979."

Gary's journal entry of June 30, like Kay's and Sue's, mentions each of the points he elaborated on in his presentation to the class. In the journal, he wrote, "Not only do we dispose of nuclear waste in poor ways but also animals can carry toxic material for many miles themselves." Gary detailed these two points in the debate:

At the Sylvania River facilities in South Carolina, [nuclear wastes] lie in . . . carbon steel tanks, which . . . after 50 years . . . develop cracks through which more than 43,000 gallons of high-level waste leak into the soil. . . . Also, when we . . . expose the soil . . . animals dig around and some of them get into it like a jackrabbit. Say he eats something that has nuclear sewage on it and he carries it so many more miles. Here comes a coyote or a hawk and kills that jackrabbit, and they find these other hawks and coyotes dead—killed.

Gary's journal entry asked, "will we ever be safe from radiation from nuclear waste? the answer is no" (6/30). In the debate, he elaborated: "Between 1946 and 1970, U.S. military encased 47,555 gallon drums of low-level waste in concrete-lined steel drums and dumped them into the Pacific. . . . Well now about 36 miles outside of San Francisco, one third of those drums are . . . leaking." The last sentence of Gary's entry anticipates the dramatic rhetoric with which he introduced his position to the group. The journal entry concludes: "So prepare yourself for what the year 2000 has in store for nuclear power." Gary was one of three students who followed Weber's directive to take the roles of power-company board members. (Most recited their arguments in the roles of students directing most information to their teacher.) As did Jim and Beth, Gary addressed his audience in the second person, as his "colleagues." He began his presentation by writing "MAD" [mutual assured destruction] on the board. Then he turned to the group and said to Weber (the "chairman of the board"), "As you heard, [some of] our colleagues are MAD about nuclear power." Like Kay and Sue, Gary also contributed to Weber's connuclear list. His contribution: "Ineffective ways of getting rid of waste."

Gary, Sue, Kay, Beth, Scott, and Dixie used their journals to help them prepare for what they said in class, but they didn't use these entries as their speech text; most students spoke to the group from notebooks. However, Jim, the leader of the con group, listed in his journal the points he intended to make. They are as follows:

> *PRO'S*   *"COAL"*

1. Est. *Reserve* = 650 B Tons
2. Total Resources = 10 Trillion Ton
3. US has 30% of World *coal*
   A) Economic *trade* advantage for USA
   B) Lobby Gov. towards research Subsidie regarding Syn.-fuels,

              a.   Liquification (liquid gas)

   Synfuels   b.   Gasification (gas)

              c.   Technology does exist currently
   C) [left blank]

Then, as the transcript shows, Jim spoke directly from this list:

> There's a couple of things I guess I'd like to address and clean up. First of all, regarding resources of coal, we have estimated reserves right now of 650 billion tons. We have

enough to support the United States alone for 200 years burning coal. Total resources are estimated at ten trillion tons. The economic advantage, I think, in pursuit of utilizing coal is that the United States alone has 30 percent of the estimated reserves in the world. Obviously that would give us a tremendous economic advantage as far as international trade. We do have the technology, it does exist regarding synthetic fuels, regarding liquid gas and gasification of coal. Granted, the gasification process is not as hot burning as natural gas, but I feel confident the technology exists and will continue to improve to get to the point that it will make it competitive.

Jim also contributed three points to the con list: "Total resources/tonnage of coal available," "Public Sentiment" [opposed to nuclear energy development] and "Technology for synthetic fuels." In the rebuttal discussion, Jim elaborated on several of the points noted in his journal and presented to class. In the journal, he noted "Coal Burning" and under that "Remove sulphur content w/ scrubbers." During an exchange about air pollution generated with resumption of coal burning, Jim said, "We're not talking about putting coal in the basements of houses again; we're talking about the generation of electricity, which is the most quality form of energy." Later, he countered Jill's comment that "[more than] six people each year die as a result of [coal mining accidents]" with "more than that died at Chernobyl."

Jim's journal provided him with two more of the points he raised during the rebuttal discussion, the second of which led Weber to bring the activity to a close. When Carole brought up the issue of nuclear plant construction costs, Jim supplemented her argument against nuclear plant development with reference to information noted in his journal about nuclear and coal-fired plant construction schedules (he had noted "6–10 years to construct coal plant" and "9–12 years for nuclear plant"). Then when Weber mentioned the decommissioning costs of nuclear plants, Jim raised another point, noted in his journal, about the politics of fossil fuel development. He had written: "Lobby Gov. toward research subsidy"; in class he asked, "Would you say that the money in oil as far as lobbying and politicians has a great impact on the direction the utility companies take? I mean the lack of subsidies right now [for alternative energy sources] because of low oil prices?" Jim's point here prompted Weber to discuss the idea with which he closed this activity: board members have to respond to political and economic as well as environmental concerns.

In the nuclear power debate students did much more talking than they had in any other class. The class transcript of July 1 shows students' voices for approximately 40 percent of the two-hour period; typically students talked for less than five percent of class time. During the debate proper, all of the students (whether or not they had used their journals to help them prepare) spoke for about five minutes each. Four of the students who had used their journals, however, did most of the talking during the rebuttal activity, and thus they had a greater influence on the process and outcome of this activity than did the four students who did not use their journals. Although their journal keeping was only one of many influences on Jim, Beth, Kay, and Scott's interaction with Weber and with each other, it appears to have had a significant role in promoting discussion. There was no precedent for this kind of discussion in "Spaceship Earth," but there was a precedent for using journals to prompt students to contribute to Weber's presentation. Some students may have used their journals in the debate because they had used them in exchanges with Professor Weber once before, during the in-class writing activity I describe below.

Teacher-Initiated Interaction: In-Class Journal Writing Journal keeping was explicitly made a part of classroom activities in "Spaceship Earth" on one occasion. A day after the midway point of the semester, Weber brought to class a "common ordinary incandescent" light bulb. He identified what it was made of and where its component minerals, metals, and alloys are produced. He asked students to write for five minutes in their journals about the "significance" of his discussion, and then he solicited responses from the class. He listed these responses on the blackboard.

This exercise was intended to give students an opportunity to use writing in this class not only to take notes, but also to think, reflect, and make connections. Furthermore, by inviting students to share their responses with the class, and by transcribing their responses on the board, Weber interacted with his students in what appeared to be a new way. Rather than taking notes on Weber's material, students were invited to inform Weber while he, in effect, took notes on their ideas. Thus journal keeping on this occasion was intended to prompt students to take an active role in the class agenda and to take responsibility for constructing the meaning of the subject under consideration. Although in reading from their journal entries in class, students took a more extensive part in negotiating the significance of this activity than they had in any activity thus far, Weber used their responses to direct them toward the significance that he had in mind. Although Weber told the group that there was no one "right" answer, the class transcript and journal entries suggest that Weber's interpretation was the one that counted.

Saying, "I want talk about resources by talking about and considering the lowly light bulb," Weber drew a light bulb on the board. As he identified its parts and the materials they're made of, he asked students the mineral composition of certain parts. After making these lists, he returned to each, identifying where each component mineral or resource is found. In constructing this picture of the widely distributed resources that comprise a light bulb, Weber involved students by asking them closed or leading questions:

Weber: OK, glass, what's that made of?

Jim: Silicon?

Weber: Yeah, we have glass sand, silica sand, what else?

With no immediate response, Weber answered this question: "Lime is often added and . . . feldspars."

The next interaction between Weber and students followed the same pattern. Weber asked questions intended to lead students to produce his preconceived answers:

Weber: OK, so we've got the envelope taken care of, how about this metal base, what does that look like it's made of?

Carole: Something light colored.

Weber: Yeah, light colored, not rusty, this is an aluminum base. . . . Where does the aluminum come from?

Tina: Ore?

Weber: Yeah, what do we call the ore? Anybody have any idea what it's called? It's a mixture of clays called bauxite. . . .

To better lead students toward the correct answer, Weber gave hints:

Weber: OK, down here we've got a spot of solder. What is solder? What's it made of? . . . Is it anything on the periodic table?

Carole: Is it lead?

Weber: Well, it's got lead in it. . . . It's an alloy of lead and tin.

Weber's answer to this question gave the student who answered his next question a clue:

Weber: Down here . . . the solder is connected to a little brass cap so that little metal at the bottom there is brass. What is brass? What is brass?

Mike: Is it an alloy?

Weber: That's also an alloy . . . out of what?

Weber involved his students in identifying the resources which comprise the light bulb, but he answered his own questions about the locations of these resources:

Where do [ferro alloys] come from? Well, the iron itself came from mostly the . . . upper midwest. Chromium is one of the metals which we don't have . . . where does it come from? Oh, it comes from places like South Africa. . . . We also get some from the USSR and Cuba. . . . Manganese, vanadium, where do we get that stuff? . . . Much of those are also imported. . . .

After identifying the sources of most of the components he listed, Weber introduced the writing exercise:

kind of interesting . . . at this point you're saying, Oh my gosh what's he getting to? I want you to consider this, I want you to take out a piece of paper or your journal . . . and look at the stuff here and contemplate what I've said about the light bulb. . . . What's the meaning of what I've put up here?

This was intended as a journal writing exercise, but as many as half the students didn't have their journals with them. Although the assignment handout distributed on the first day of class directed students to bring their journals with them every day because Weber would ask to see them, he had yet to do so. (The course was over half finished.) Weber realized students might not have anticipated needing their journals: he instructed them either to do the writing in their journals or to "convert" what they wrote to journal entries later.

During class on the 24th, nine students wrote responses to Weber's question in their journals during class. Their entries average 65 words; none is more than five sentences. Five of these entries are titled with the question Weber wrote on the board: "WHAT IS THE SIGNIFICANCE OF THE LIGHTBULB?" In six of the nine, most of the entry repeats or summarizes what Weber told the class when he identified the components of the light bulb. For example, his comment that we take the light bulb for granted is reiterated in Sue's entry: "It's amazing how much we depend on the light bulb even though the only time we really appreciate them is after they've burned out . . . ," in Kay's "the light itself is so much taken for granted," and Howard's "it is hardly ever thought about." Weber's point that the light bulb comprises elements mined in various countries throughout the world is recounted in Howard's entry: "The light bulb is made up of many different materials from many places," and in Carole's "A light bulb has the significance of being a conglomerate of minerals or resources in order to supply a society with electricity. These resources are not produced here in the U.S.; they are distributed through the world." Likewise, Scott wrote, "the light bulb uses so many different elements from so many countries" (Scott and Howard both make this point twice), and Sue concurred: "The actual bulb is made up of so many different elements!"

With only five minutes to write, students had little time to draw inferences from the material they reiterated. In most of the entries written in class, the implication that international affairs are affected by global distribution of mineral resources received a phrase or, at most, a couple of sentences. Carole concluded her first paragraph with "[these resources] are distributed through the world, therefore, the U.S. must 'import' those minerals to produce a simple light bulb." Scott's entry begins, "The lightbulb is a product that can only be produced by cooperation of many different country's," but he dropped this idea, to reiterate Weber's point that "the lightbulb uses so many different elements from so many countries." After expressing surprise, as did many others, at the complexity of the bulb ("It is amazing that we take some resources and produce something like the light bulb"), Gary began his next paragraph, "It is also important to get very important resources from other countries. So maybe the United States should keep good relations with other countries." Only three of the entries that were written during class (before the significance of the light bulb was discussed) introduce and sustain attention over more than a couple of sentences to the sociopolitical implication that, as John puts it, "countries must interact through trade."

Not surprisingly, when Weber asked the group to tell him how they responded to this question, three of the six items he listed on the board reiterated or reflected his introduction to the exercise. Kay, who had written that she was "fascinated by the content of the bulb," told Weber that she thought it was "interesting how complex they are, given the small size," whereupon he wrote on the board "EVEN SIMPLE DEVICES ARE COMPLEX." A few minutes later, Kay contributed another, related point: "I . . . think the combining of different minerals is really interesting . . . in what they form." To this, Weber responded, "Making of alloys and so on" as he wrote "ALLOYS ARE INTERESTING" on the blackboard. (As he did so, he said "You obviously have an engineering bent," and the class laughed.) Carole, reading from her journal, told Weber that "The electricity that is produced is something that a society could do without; however, most of us are unwilling to make that sacrifice for the sake of a better standard of living"; Weber then wrote "ONE COULD DO WITHOUT" on the board.

Weber told students when he solicited their contributions that "there's no one answer." He took the role of secretary as students dictated the items on the lists of significances. His goal for this exercise, he told me, was "to get them thinking about this . . . and contribute something to class." Although the first point on his list ("DEPENDENCE UPON THE REST OF THE WORLD," contributed by Beth) was directly related to the kind of significance he was getting to, Weber didn't use this item to draw conclusions: closing off students' contributions at this early point in the "discussion" would subvert his goals for the activity. Instead he paraphrased and edited students' subsequent contributions, shaping them in the direction of what Weber had said he anticipated getting to. For example, he corrected a contribution that conflicted with his intentions for this list. In his journal, Jim had written that "it is obvious from our discussion that the resources incorporated into the light bulb require a balance of trade with particular countries to provide those resources." Jim contributed this to the discussion activity by saying, "Well, there's a balance of trade with other countries." Weber responded, "Balance of trade or international trade?" As he said this, Weber wrote "INTERNATIONAL TRADE" on the board.

To close in on a point he used to conclude this activity, Weber similarly edited Jim's second contribution. In a follow-up to his first point, Jim said, "I was going to say that the disbursement of minerals around the world doesn't allow anyone a monopoly, it forces sharing." As Jim said the last phrase in that sentence, "it forces sharing," Weber began to write "NOT EVENLY DISTRIB-UTED." As he started to write, Weber said, "Not evenly distributed, can I say that?" Weber then used this point to segue into an inference that uneven mineral distribution has sociopolitical implications. With my assistance (I offered that "I think our use of chromium is interesting in light of the reluctance to impose trade sanctions on South Africa"), Weber then asked rhetorically if students thought "the fact that South Africa supplies about a good half of the metals we import has any relationship to the administration's reluctance to totally ban imports . . . from South Africa." Weber concluded this activity, and the day's class, by saying that "this is one of the areas where geologic reality [of] uneven distribution of minerals . . . gets into moral, political, social ideas and events. . . . There are connections between these problems."

Under pressure of time, ("By the time he said 'stop,' Tina told me, "I was maybe halfway through the first sentence"), students wrote little in their journals that was not related to the point they anticipated Weber was looking for. Beth said that "I figured out . . . from [the beginning of the exercise] that he was going to try to show us the interaction of all these components, what else would you use the light bulb for." Tina told me that "he was trying to make us realize what the government is thinking when they don't . . . have sanctions." Jim wrote that "It is obvious from our discussion that the resources incorporated into the light bulb require a balance of trade with particular countries to provide those resources." Others, like Tina, had already thought about this issue: "before he started talking about anything . . . I was thinking about our dependence . . . I had thought of that before we started discussing the significance in class."

Most of the responses to Weber's question that were written after class or that were later "converted," as Weber put it, into journal entries, either summarize or otherwise recount the significances that were established in class. Students' comments to me about this exercise suggest that there were differences of opinion about the moral and political ramifications of Weber's concluding observations, but they were not pursued. (Jill, for example, told me that "we had better be nice to South Africa," but Darryl—who wasn't in class on the 24th—told me later that our relations with South Africa are dictated not by resource availability, but by racism. Neither of these points was expressed in journal entries.) In the light bulb significance activity, journal keeping was intended to give students a greater say than they had had in class thus far, and Weber said he hoped students would develop their own independent interpretations of his material in journal entries. Nonetheless, the writing and the interaction it prompted served to develop and confirm the authority of Weber's message and his method of conveying it.

The foregoing discussion may give a false impression of the numbers of entries used in exchanges among students and professor. The entries cited above represent less than five percent (19) of the total number (298) written for this class. Of 38 class hours, fewer than 2 1/2 were given to exchanges or activities in which journal keeping played a role. Weber did not indicate that students' participation in class would "count." What did count, for almost their total grade, was performance on tests. This is one reason that students used their journals as study guides in the ways described below.

Preparing for Tests   Testing was established as a central feature of "Spaceship Earth" on the first day of class, when Weber introduced course procedures by advising students that they ought to make a habit of attending class: the first of three multiple-choice exams was "coming up this Friday." Weber spent ten minutes explaining his plans for calculating scores, but his discussion of evaluation did not include advice about how students ought to study or about what, specifically, they would be tested on. With the exception of two brief exchanges (on June 16 and 26) during which students asked Weber what the second and third tests would cover, and 20 minutes of discussion (on July 2) of a final exam review sheet, class time was not given to activity intended to help students prepare for tests. Without much information, then, about how much of the lecture and textbook material they would need to study (or how they would need to know it), many students used their journals as well as their class notes to help them prepare for tests. Although they were not assigned to use journals as study aids (and Weber told me later he planned to discourage future classes from doing so), three students rewrote their class notes, and outlined or summarized Weber's lectures in their journals. Others, after the first and second tests, used their journals to reflect on their performance and anticipate or report on study strategies for the next exam.

Of the students who used journals to help them remember Weber's material, Jill went to the most trouble. She told me that her procedure in writing entries was to "open [her] notebook and start going through" what Weber lectured on. Then, in her journal, she reported everything she "fe[lt] was important" from her notes. As she put it in her June 11 entry, her purpose in making entries was to "understand all of [what we learned in class] better . . . to think about it, organize my thoughts and write down the material in my own words." She also occasionally recopied Weber's blackboard sketches, but for the most part, Jill said, she tried to explain "what the drawing[s were] about." Although Jill sometimes reiterated Weber verbatim in her journal, she typically paraphrased his material, making narratives of her notebook references to processes Weber explained. On June 13, for example, Jill's class notes give a shorthand version of Weber's explanation of the production of soil, referring to parts of this process in the order he mentioned them. In her notes, she copied Weber's sketch of a landform profile titled "Sedimentary rocks." On the sketch she identified various sedimentary rocks; off to the right side she wrote "weathering is occurring—breakdown of rocks by the elements." Under that: "1) physical—physical breakdown of rock—collision, frost action." And "2) Chemical— chemical breakdown of minerals." On the next page, under a sketch titled "Burying Soil," Jill wrote, "soil is formed by weather of rocks, rain moves the soil down beginning of *erosion*. Now in transport, water is the most import thing (wind, too, glacier/ice) is ultimately deposited."

In her journal entry for June 13, Jill narrated the process she had noted and illustrated in fragmentary form:

> The stuff that comes down the mountain and settles in the valleys or dips is called soil and that contains pieces of rock that are disintegrated. The mountain and the land surface is weathered constantly to make the soil. There are two ways: Physical weathering (physical breakdown of rock, collisions, frost action, etc.) Chemical weathering (chemical breakdown of minerals, reactions between elements and

compounds, growths, etc.) Soil is formed by the weathering of the rocks.

Not surprisingly, Jill correctly answered the two questions on the first exam that pertained to weathering and soil production. Using her journal entries to define and explain geological concepts—coalification, the law of superposition, pyroclastics, subduction zones, or the rock cycle, to give a few examples—helped Jill answer test questions requiring identification of terms and concepts that Weber had emphasized in his lectures.

Like Jill, John L. also used his journal to fix in his mind Weber's definitions. On June 13, before giving the first exam, Weber had charted on the blackboard the subtypes and formation processes of igneous, metamorphic, and sedimentary rocks. Terms Weber had underlined while constructing this chart are reiterated in John's journal entry for the 13th. This entry concludes:

> Intrusive—Plutonic—is magma that doesn't make it to the surface. Extrusive—Volcanic is magma that does make it to the surface . . . consolidated is sedimentary rocks that are cemented together. Examples are: shale, siltstone, sandstone, conglomerated.

By linking terms and descriptors in this way, John memorized potentially useful test information. Using journal entries to outline or itemize Weber's material was probably one of the strategies that earned John a high score on all three tests.

In addition to outlining lectures as a test preparation strategy, students also used journals to anticipate what or how they would study differently next time. After the first exam, several students reported in their journals that they had misjudged the time and energy they needed to put into studying. Gary wrote in his 6/15 entry, "Well after the first test I know how much more I need to study. . . . I could have studied a lot harder than I did." Gary's response to the first test was shared by Scott, who wrote on 6/13, "Next test I'm going to have to study more"; and by Jill, whose June 15 entry reports, "I'll try harder next time." Beth and Carole faulted their test-taking process; Beth blamed herself for "reading one thing and writing another," and Carole, for "selecting my answers too hastily because of the time allowance." John and Sue anticipated better luck on the next test because, as John put it (addressing Weber), he "found out what questions you ask" (6/16). Sue also wrote, "At least [I know] now what to expect on the remaining two exams." Others indicated that they would make more use of the textbook in studying for the second test. Karen, for example, wrote she would "spend more time in the book" (6/20); Carole, that she had "miscalculated by thinking more questions would be taken from the class notes" (6/16); Jill reported on June 16 that she had "read 4 . . . chapters for the next test."

After the first and second exams, Tina, Sue, and John explained in their journals what they missed—Tina to "correct mistakes," she told me; Sue and John to justify their errors. Tina had picked the wrong answer to a question on the first exam that began, "The chain of islands we call Hawaii is caused by." In her June 16 journal entry, she corrected her wrong answer, writing that "The Hawaiian Islands are on a hot spot not a subduction zone or a mid-oceanic ridge . . . notice that the islands that are farthest from the hot spot are also the smallest." Sue, in her journal entry for June 16, claimed that "the way that question about half-life was worded really threw me for a loop." (Six others missed the half-life question, which read, in part: "The half-life of a radioactive substance is: a) half the time it takes for all the substance to decay b) time for half the substance to decay. . . . d) half the time it takes for half the original quantity to decay.") After the second exam, John wrote in his journal that "The question I missed was, 'What causes volcanoes in the NW United States?' I had it narrowed down to subduction zones and none of the above. I thought it was none of the above because I thought that it was just a fault line, not really a subduction zone" (6/23).

Several students reported that, after the first exam, they had a better idea of what Weber's tests were like. They weren't sure, though, as they studied for the second test, whether they would be responsible for textbook chapters on material Weber hadn't yet addressed in his lectures. Journal references to performance on the second exam reflect this uncertainty: Kay, for example, wrote on June 23 that she "should have asked for sure whether chapter ten would be on the test on Friday." Carole reported in her entry of the 23rd that she "felt confident until [she] discovered [she] reviewed a wrong chapter and omitted the other." Jill wrote that she "didn't expect the questions on waves and wave energy." Similar confusion about what would be covered is expressed in Sue's analysis of her performance: "I understood that we were not going to be tested over the flooding and coastal hazards, so 3 out of 8 I missed for the simple reason that I was unfamiliar with the material" (6/23).

In accounting for their performance on the second test, several journal writers may have been psychologically preparing themselves for the final: Gary wrote, for example, that "if I would have better understood the questions I might have done better. But I must look ahead and try to get the last exam" (6/23). Carole wrote that expressing her frustrations about her test performance helped her "vent" them: "I feel better . . . being able to vent my feelings in writing" (6/23). (She told me later that writing down how frustrated and angry she felt "sometimes makes it easier to concentrate on studying.") Carole, Sue, and Kay noted study plans for the final. Sue reported that she "spent a large portion of my afternoon reading the text and preparing for the final. . . . I have a good start on the study guide handout." Carole wrote, "This weekend I intend to spend a great deal of my time studying," and Kay "[thought she] underst[ood] the components [she had] been studying" (7/2). Beth advised herself to "stop overanalyzing test questions" (6/23).

Despite the evidence that some students used journals as a "study guide" (so described to me by Tina and Jill), those who rewrote their class notes in their journals or reported on study strategies and plans did not (with John's exception) receive higher scores than those who said they studied only from their notes and textbooks. One reason their journals didn't give students much help in preparing for tests was that journal keeping and test taking were understood to be fundamentally different activities. As Jill told me, journal keeping was for "thinking," testing for "remembering names and [concepts] and then put[ting] them together in the right way." Most students were less interested in terms and concepts per se than they were in the applications of geological literacy to their own lives that Weber pointed out in many of his presentations. (After Weber's lectures on landsliding and mass movement, for example, three students referred in their journals to Weber's explanation of landslide physics; nine responded to his anecdotes about the follies of home building in geologically uncertain areas.) Students knew they were responsible for learning the definitions of terms and concepts, but Weber's demonstrations, illustrations, anecdotes, jokes, and sound effects were, for many, more entertaining and memorable than the theoretical information about geological processes intended to be the "basis" for practical material. (Weber himself distinguished "academic" from "real-world" geology on several occasions.) As I will suggest later in this chapter, many journal writers were troubled by a disjunction between what they were learning from Weber and what they were being tested on. Because they enjoyed and learned from Weber's lectures, and because they used class time to listen to Weber and not, for the most part, to communicate with him, students did so in their journals, using them to express their interest in and their difficulties with his class.

Responding to Class Activities   "Today we discussed," "today's topic was," "today we went over," "we are starting [earthquakes, or volcanoes, or hazards]": these phrases or their variants occur in more than 200 of the journal entries, introducing as many as half of them. Professor Weber did not assign his students to respond in their journals to the events of "Spaceship Earth," but he indicated they could do so when he showed them entries that reported on, reviewed, and raised questions about his lectures and tests. For reasons I will suggest as I conclude this chapter, all of Weber's students used their journals to respond to their instructor's material or to his methods of presenting it. Most of these responses were affirmative; a few (perhaps ten percent of the total) were negative. Many journal writers affirmed Weber's conduct of the course by expressing interest in his material or praising his methods. Others affirmed the authority of Weber's message by adopting his rhetoric or his point of view, or by referring to what they learned from his lectures or the activities he conducted. As Weber predicted on the first day of class, criticism of the course—in challenges to Weber's information, complaints about his methods, or recommendations for change was typically "balanced," as he put it, by praise.

Affirmation   All of Weber's students, some in as many as 75 percent of their entries, expressed interest in the subjects of their teacher's lectures. Most of the direct expressions of interest are responses to what John called the most "dramatic" of Weber's topics. Among those inspired, for example, by Weber's explanation and illustration (on the first day of class) of "How big is big and how old is old?" were Carole, who wrote, "The most interesting thing I learned today was about the size comparison of the earth to the universe" (6/10); Scott, who wrote, "It was really interesting to hear about the size and age of the universe" (6/10);

and Tina, who wrote, "details . . . I thought were interesting [included] . . . what exactly is a quasar?" (6/10). The evolution of the continents interested John K., who wrote he "thought that continental drift was really a fascinating topic" (6/11); and Karen: "Your lecture on plate tectonics was interesting and informative" (6/11). Earthquakes and volcanoes (topics John called "more dramatic than ground water") also provoked a response which six journal keepers used the word "interest" to describe. Among them were Kay, who wrote that "The volcano and earthquake discussions are really interesting" (6/11). Many were surprised to learn from Weber in class on June 11 that the potentially active fault which caused this country's worst earthquake (the 1885 New Madrid quake that changed the course of the Mississippi) "runs under most of Iowa." About this, Carole wrote on June 11 that she "learned an especially interesting fact about Iowa today," and Beth concurred: "I find it very interesting that there is a fault under Iowa" (6/11).

In connection with expressing interest in Weber's material, many writers praised Weber's enthusiasm, his knowledge, and his skill at explaining his material. Carole wrote that "my instructor has a unique way of explaining things in a logical, easy to understand way. Fortunately, [Carl] has the ability to explain a vast amount and . . . complex material at a novice level, which is one of the main reasons I'm learning and as interested in environmental geology as I am" (6/11). Kay indicated the extent to which she valued Weber's explanations when she wrote that "I was anxious to hear you describe the chapter because I needed to get it clearer" (6/13). Jill wrote that "your demonstrations to explain the laws of gravity . . . friction and sliding . . . and resisting forces . . . made the ideas more tangible" (6/18). Carole, pointing out that Weber was one of only a few of her instructors to "use all of the blackboard," praised his "detailed explanations along with visual aids [that] reinforce [the] topic" (6/27). Sue complimented Weber on the blackboard sketches with which he illustrated different kinds of landslides (6/19).

Twelve students praised Weber's anecdotes in their journals. In his June 19 entry, John, for example, appreciated Weber's narrative and visual illustrations of homebuilding on cliffs: "talking about the physics of landslides and how they occur wasn't that interesting, but when it's tied in with peoples' experience it makes it easier to digest." Three times during the course, Weber took time from the published agenda (the course syllabus) to show slides, some of which depicted him in difficult situations (sliding off the side of a cliff, for example) that he described with amusement. These slide presentations were warmly reviewed by ten students, in 14 of their journal entries.

Several writers implicitly expressed their interest in Weber's material by adopting his rhetoric, his point of view, or both. After Weber's lecture on avalanches on June 19, for example, Jill repeated in her journal—almost verbatim—a warning he gave the class: "when skiing—avoid avalanche shoots—stay in trees, stay on top and watch warnings" (6/19). In her next entry, written after a lecture on waste disposal, she adopted Weber's rhetoric again: "don't use sinkholes as dumps." Scott similarly reiterated Weber's injunction that "strip mining makes a mess of the land!" (6/26). In class on June 11, Weber said he had "reservations about the Big Bang." So did Dixie, who wrote that "I find I have reservations about the Big Bang," (6/20) and Jill, for whom "the Big Bang is too limited" (6/20). Jim was among the writers who acknowledged Weber as his source, prefacing a June 27 comment about current events—"the direction in which Bonnie ultimately approaches land is somewhat unpredictable"—with "as we discuss in class." (By "we," Jim told me, he meant Weber.)

Paraphrasing or reiterating what Weber said was one way journal writers communicated their interest in his material; referring to what they were learning from him was another. Dixie and Gary referred abstractly to what they learned from the course: Dixie wrote that "Taking this course has opened my eyes in many ways" (6/20); for Gary, "It seems this class has something to offer everyday. I can look at the environment and better understand why it's like it is" (6/16). Others referred to specific topics. Tina, for example, "had really never thought about where all the elements come from" (6/11), and Roger had "not thought about the concept of continental drift . . . since [his] freshman class in high school" (6/11). Nor had Kay, who reported that "there is so much about volcanoes I don't know." For John K., "thinking about mountains actually being formed now was something I'd never thought about" (6/11); and Kay wrote that she "felt excited because I was understanding [how the continents formed]. This is one of few times in a science course when I've felt like I could explain these theories and patterns to other people" (6/11). Carole remarked in her June 10 entry that she "did not know before today . . . that we are not the only universe. I thought 'universe' meant one."

Others, like Carole, referred to a change in their understanding. After Weber's demonstration of landsliding physics on June 11, John K. wrote that "viscosity was what I kept hearing in that motor oil commercial and never knew what it was. I do now" (6/11). Beth responded in her journal to Weber's June 16 introduction to geologic hazards with "I had no idea we live on such an unstable footing. You hear of such stuff but to see someone who has studied it and knows what they are talking about discuss it . . . makes it real" (6/16). About Weber's lecture on mass movement, Darryl reflected that "only now do I understand why and how avalanches happen" (6/19), and Beth exclaimed, "How about that! I always thought trees are curved like that to catch the sun" (6/16). After the field trip to the cemetery, four students reported in their June 12 entries that their understanding of rocks had changed. Howard wrote that he "will never look at rocks the same ways again"; Scott was "learning to really appreciate the beauty of rocks"; and John K. "had a better concept of what a rock is and what it is made up of. Instead of just thinking of it as something you get caught between the tread of your tire."

Eight students reported that they were enlightened by Weber's advice about the early warning signals of earthquakes, avalanches, and other forms of "mass movement." After writing that he had "learned more about the universe in the last week and a half than [I] even thought [I] knew before," Gary concluded that he "always thought it would be great to have a house in the hills but after your tips I think I . . . might change my mind" (6/19). Howard wrote that Weber had "talked [him] out of moving to California" (6/19); John K. that he would "remember how to tell [if a potential home construction site] is in danger of landsliding . . . [which] I wouldn't have paid much attention to before. I'll also know what to do if I ever get caught in an avalanche" (6/19). Scott wrote that "If an earthquake ever happened . . . I now know what to do," (6/18) and Carole noted that knowing how to react in an earthquake "may prove beneficial" (6/18).

Students not only said that they found Weber's advice useful, they also said they admired the roles he described himself taking in issues involving environmental hazards. His position, for example, in a local controversy about the disposition of hazardous wastes elicited praise from several journal writers. As advisor to a local citizens' committee opposed to hazardous chemical dumping, Weber took an unpopular stand when he advocated building a containment facility instead of hauling the waste chemicals elsewhere. Darryl wrote, "I agree with you totally in that John Deere toxic waste disposal issue" (6/27). Jill, after writing that she "learned a lot about our landfill," went on to complain about the "lack of responsible action" and to compliment Weber on his position (6/27); Carole observed that she "respecte[ed] a person who has the initiative to take a stand for what they believe in rather than be sujected to group think . . . after today I must admit to being an uninformed citizen" (6/27).

References to change in understanding or in opinions are scattered through journal entries, but after the nuclear energy debate, six of nine entries which address the activity are wholly devoted to what the writers learned from it and how their views had changed. Students' changed viewpoints reflect Weber's opinion that despite its advantages over coal burning, nuclear energy has become prohibitively expensive. Sue wrote, "nuclear power has a lot more factors against it than for it" (7/1). Jim agreed: "After doing some research and listening to debate, I am firmly convinced our technology does not exist to support [cost efficient] nuclear plant construction" (7/1). Tina reported that "Doing my research for the pro-side (which was not easy) I learned a lot about the different types of nuclear plants and how they are built and the processes they use . . . in the long run I found more reasons to be anti-nuke" (7/11). Others' journal entries reflect Weber's concluding observation that the issue is more complex than it might appear: Gary, for example, noted that "I think doing the debate has helped me understand that nuclear power is a very sensitive issue" (7/1). Weber had suggested that decision makers' positions are influenced not only by specifically environmental concerns, but also by the politics of energy production and consumption. Kay observed that it "depends on your perspective whether you are more interested in costs or environmental hazards. . . . I bet each book that all of us read . . . showed varying statistics" (7/2). In responses to the debate, as in responses to the light bulb significance exercise, students reported and elaborated on issues that they raised in speaking to each other. Nonetheless, many of their observations reflect Weber's concluding analysis of the issues.

Journal writers also supported Weber's agenda by following up on his invitations to ask him questions in class. Weber typically concluded his discussion of particular topics by inviting questions. Journal entries show all students had questions; only a few asked them in class, however. For fear, Carole suggested, of "looking stupid," or because, as Beth speculated, students "didn't want to take up time when who knows . . . [what their questions] could lead to" (questions might lead Weber away from material he would test them on), many students suppressed their questions, raising them after class in their journals. As Weber finished his June 10 lecture on the Big Bang, for example, he prefaced a request for questions with "If the Big Bang doesn't confuse you, there's something wrong. . . . Even physicists are confused about it." Ten students who said nothing in class expressed confusion in their journal entries for June 10. "I don't understand how the universe could have been compressed to the size of a dot, it just is impossible to begin to comprehend," wrote Scott. For John K., it was "hard to grasp the idea of the universe having an outer boundary." For Gary, "It seems like when I start with how it first started and then put it together with how it came into being, I get lost." Howard thought "matter must have existed before the explosion." Dixie asked, "If indeed this theory is correct, where does God come in?" Roger also "[found] it . . . difficult to accept the 'Big Bang' theory and subsequent formation of life on earth without making room for the consideration of divine intervention." Sue wondered, "What was the hot mass [that blew up and began the formation of galaxies]? Do scientists know its size or shape? Where did this mass come from? It all seems unclear to me." Kay had "many questions after today's lecture. I don't want to sound stupid . . . but could the planets have been stars if they had more hydrogen in them?"

Journal writers not only responded to Weber's calls for questions, they also responded to his requests for personal experience anecdotes like those he told them. All of Weber's lectures involved description of his government, military, or academic experience of the geological processes he explained. Many of his stories illustrated the danger of unwise development, the mismanagement of resources, or discrepancies between academic and "real world" geology. Many of his stories turned out to be jokes at his or his colleagues' expense. At the beginning of class on June 18, Weber asked, "Anybody have any good stories?" Nobody responded in class (perhaps because I said, "That's your department, [Carl]"), but five entries dated the 18th (and more than 40 written at various times throughout the course) narrated or alluded to personal experiences of the sort Weber often told the class. In an entry dated 6/18 that concludes with a comment on the allure of danger, Jim described his excitement when thunderstorms approach. Darryl wrote about his experience helping victims of a preventable flood. Sue wrote this in her June 18 entry:

Whenever I hear someone talking about a Richter scale, one particular thing comes to mind. . . . When my little sister was studying about earthquakes in her physical science class in about third or fourth grade, she came home one day and asked, "Mom, do we have a Richter scale?" As if everyone owns one!

Weber's puns, jokes, deliberately misdrawn sketches, and facetious responses to students were often admired in the journals. "[Carl], you seemed extremely humorous today," wrote Carole after Weber gave a lecture on avalanches (6/16) that included an anecdote about buried skiers (each named after a "Spaceship Earth" student) who didn't know they could spit to tell which way was up. About this lecture, Sue wrote, "I think your illustrations . . . are hilarious. . . . Seriously, though, are you really supposed to spit to determine which way is up? Wouldn't the snow be packed so tight around you that you still wouldn't be able to tell how to get out by looking at it?" (6/18). Weber's puns on the names and concepts he explained—schist, gneiss, mass movement, for example—were a reason Beth suggested in her journal that Weber would probably tell her petrified wood was "scared," and that Howard wrote, "Your inspirational lecture [on earthquakes] really shook me up! (Oh, no! I've been listening to you too much!!)." Weber made many self-deprecating references to his baldness; in her journal, Beth similarly deprecated her physique when she wrote that "if you look at my back around my waist you'll see . . . those solifluction lobes he drew on the board" (6/19).

Critique The majority of entries support Weber's message and his method of conveying it: his students appreciated their teacher's skill at explaining his subject in funny and easy-to-understand ways. However, not all students were satisfied with their limited role in negotiating the course agenda; many used their journals to register dissatisfaction with the design or management of activities (for example, exams and the debate) and assignments (journal keeping) used to evaluate their performance in the course. Although Weber was widely perceived to be accessible and friendly, his students occasionally criticized him for failing to clearly communicate his expectations of them. As I indicated earlier in this chapter, Carole's journal shows that exchanges with Weber pertaining to test material failed to provide her with the specific direction she wanted. Several other journal entries reflect their authors' frustration that Weber misunderstood or evaded their questions in class. On June 18, for example, Beth had asked Weber in class if "the ground opens up" during earthquakes; Weber told her that "collapsing buildings cause the most damage," and he went on to talk about how earthquakes cause structural failure. Denied opportunity to follow up her question in class, Beth did so in her journal that night: "If the land doesn't really open then where do they get the photos of cars . . . hanging on the edge of crevices after earthquakes?" (6/18).

Most of the complaints registered in the journals pertain to difficulties with Weber's exams. In the entries they wrote after the first day of class, Karen and Carole indicated that having to remember material for the fast-approaching first exam affected their attitude toward the course: after praising Weber and expressing interest in the topics to be covered, Karen concluded, "Let's hope I feel the same way after the test" (6/9). Carole, after reporting on what particularly interested her in Weber's lecture, concluded, "However, I'm not sure I'll be able to remember some of the distances and comparison figures" (6/9). Gary hoped he would understand how the solar system originated "before it's too late!!" (6/10). Students' interest in what they learned at the cemetery about the composition and history of gravestones contrasted with their concern that this field trip hadn't helped them prepare for the test the following day. Howard wrote, "There is no way I'm going to be able to remember all of those . . . rocks! I hope that is not on the test tomorrow" (6/12). For Carole, the field trip was "too long . . . More time could have been spent in the classroom so we wouldn't have to rush through rock classifications" (6/12). For Karen, "the detail needed to fully understand" the material Weber indicated students would be responsible for "was not provided" (6/12).

Complaints after the first exam reflect students' disappointed expection that this test would evenly cover the first week's topics or that its questions would primarily be drawn from the lectures they had enjoyed and learned from. Of 45 multiple-choice test questions, three asked for information about the cosmological topics that had taken up most of the first four hours of class. Beth complained that "only a few of the test questions were what I expected. No doppler effect, [or] Hubbell . . ." (6/15). Carole was "amazed because there were no questions on the emission spectra wavelengths, colors, the doppler effect, the chronological time line or the individual planets" (6/13).

The "quick run-through of historical and physical geology" that Weber had promised for this week—the subject of four of nine class hours—provided the majority of test questions: 18 of them pertained to rock and mineral composition. Postponed by the field trip, much of Weber's explanation of this material was, as Karen put it, "crammed" into the hour before students took the exam. John complained that he "didn't like having to absorb new material in the lecture right before the test. It doesn't give you much of a chance to study or review the material" (6/13). Karen's "mind became so cluttered this morning that [she] really got thrown off" (6/13). Carole "selected [her] answers too hastily because of the time allowance" (6/13). Carole and several others also complained that they had not expected to be responsible for textbook material Weber hadn't discussed. Carole's June 13 entry concluded: "I miscalculated by thinking more questions would be taken from class notes. Overall I'm angry." So was Sue: "I was real disappointed with the test results. I had no idea there would be so many questions from the book."

Although students negotiated with Weber for more time to prepare for the second test (postponed from Friday June 20 to Monday the 23rd), their frustration with the differences between what they were learning from Weber and what they were tested on is reflected in many entries written between the first and second tests. Karen, for example, wrote after the lecture on earthquakes, "I wish I could have laughed after the last test as I laughed in class today" (6/18), and Kay "enjoyed the real life examples, but I'm afraid we might be getting carried away. . . . The last test was hard enough without worrying . . . about being rushed at the end" (6/19).

Complaints after the second exam reflect the fact that many students didn't hear Weber indicate, at the end of class a few days before the test, that it would cover textbook material he had not yet lectured on. Jill "didn't expect the questions on waves and wave energy" (6/23); Carole "didn't even study chapter ten because I figured that would be the chapter not covered" (6/23); and Kay "thought chapter 10 would be on the test, but Friday it sounded like nothing we hadn't covered would be on it" (6/23). Complaints about the test also reflect students' difficulty remembering the items of basic geological literacy—the classes of earthquake waves or the physics of sea waves, for example—that most found less interesting than Weber's application of this material in his descriptions of the impact of earthquakes and floods on human social affairs. "I have learned a lot more than my score would indicate," wrote Beth in her June 17 entry. "I just can't seem to do well and yet it's not because I don't understand the information," wrote Carole (6/23). Beth's June 23 entry suggests that Weber's second test measured, not understanding of geological processes, but "errors in comprehension" of details. Going over the test "offered a unique opportunity for us to explore the errors in our comprehension of material," she wrote. Karen recommended in her June 23 entry that Weber "ask more general questions."

Complaints about the debate as well as the test reflect students' frustration that they hadn't been prepared. Although Weber had called this activity a debate, he hadn't told students they would be asked to present their arguments from the front of the room; the only precedent for students' involvement in this class was exchanges between students and professor during which they sat in their seats and he stood at the front of the room. Furthermore, Weber drew attention to the novelty of his asking students to give speeches when he said, as he introduced the rebuttal activity, "How many of you were nervous up here?" Howard speculated in his journal that "so many people were gone today because they didn't want to have to talk in front of class. There are not too many classes where you have to do that." "As for the debate," wrote Karen:

> I was disgusted. I didn't like the idea of getting up in front of class to present each person's views. This is not a speech class. I think each side should have been on different sides of the room and treat it more like a discussion. People would have been more relaxed and willing to speak up in this setting. The rebuttals should prove this—I thought it was much easier to pay close attention and to pick out important points. People were able to speak up on a volunteer basis which meant the most important points were rebutted or first considered. My recommendation is that you require everyone to speak but let them do it on their own when they feel their points can be worked in. . . . Let it be more of a discussion. (7/1)

Carole concurred with Karen's assessment: "I for one was not prepared to handle the situation in this manner. . . . I preferred to participate in the rebuttal because it was spontaneous and I was more relaxed" (7/1). Students' complaints about journal keeping similarly reflect frustration with the management of this assignment. They expressed confusion about the purposes and audience for their writing. Sue wrote that she "didn't know what to say" (7/2); Karen, that "there isn't that much to write about" (7/2); and for Howard, "the journal was a pain the ____" (7/2). Beth, on the other hand, wrote that "I have so many thoughts about the class lesson that I am frustrated in my attempts to put them down" (6/20). Without responses from the reader who would use their writing in evaluating their performance, many students felt their journal keeping lacked direction; thus, as Karen put it on June 17, "I have to force myself to write daily so I don't get behind."

Weber's students enjoyed and learned from him, but their awareness that he would use their journals in determining their grades is a reason Kay, Carole, Sue, Karen, and others blame themselves—and not simply their teacher's methods—for their difficulty with assignments. Karen, for example, prefaced her critique of the debate by acknowledging she "doesn't like speaking in front of groups" (7/7); Sue blamed herself for not studying enough, before she suggested that Weber had not clearly indicated what the second test would cover. Although Carole, Sue, and Karen never asked Weber in my hearing how he would determine credit for the journal, after the first two tests, they were all in the C range and were not satisfied: all three wrote extra-credit papers and were likely to have hoped that their journals might win them extra points. The authors of the entries Weber had offered as models had used a predominately self-questioning and self-critical rhetoric. His summer '86 students likewise hedged their critique of their instructor with expressions of self-doubt. This seemed, after all, to be what he wanted.

As they wrote in their journals, Weber's students could be certain only of a few things: they must date each entry, they must produce 18 entries that appeared to have been written on different days, they didn't have to worry about grammar or spelling, and they had in some way to address their geology course. Because their professor had so much to tell them about, and because there was so little time, they did not ask nor were they required to negotiate much of the agenda for this course with him. Because they liked the teacher and knew he wanted them to like him, they had incentives to use their journals to try to develop rapport with him by praising his teaching and letting him know they were doing their homework. On the other hand, because they didn't know how carefully or seriously he would read their journals, they also used them, contrary to his expressed expectations, as study guides and running commentaries on his class.

I have looked in this chapter at how journal keeping served the interaction among students and professor, suggesting that it allowed and in fact encouraged them to interact with each other in what we think of as traditional ways. In other words, the teacher dominated the class and controlled the agenda, while students took down his information and attempted, in their work for him, to figure out and meet his expectations of them. Many used their journals, not for the "thoughtful reflection" on the issues that Weber's assignment called for, but as an outlet for their reactions to class. In the next two chapters, I want to consider why journal keeping worked this way by looking more closely at Professor Weber's reasons for making this assignment and at two of his students' reasons for writing as they did.

4

THE SOCIOPOLITICS
OF JOURNAL KEEPING
IN "SPACESHIP EARTH":
TWO STUDENTS

In the preceding chapter, I suggested that Weber's students used their journals for purposes other than those he assigned. Asked to reflect on connections among geological issues and their own experiences, many students nonetheless used their journals as attempts to communicate to their teacher their reactions to his instruction. I argued that, because class activities were managed in a way that minimized students' participation, many used their journals in an attempt to negotiate the class agenda or Weber's methods of evaluation. Some journal keepers seemed to be entering into a kind of one-sided conversation with Weber, commenting on what he was doing for them (for instance, explaining or entertaining) and what they were doing for him (studying or learning). Thus I interpret the journals as arenas for social interaction.

To understand what happens within these arenas, let us assume that people occupy what sociologist of education David Hargreaves calls social *positions* (Hargreaves, 1972, p. 70). These are defined by Hargreaves as "broad categories of persona with similar attributes who hold certain structured relationships with members of other positions." As I argued in Chapter 2, the positions of *teacher* or of *student* are associated with certain roles, or characteristic behaviors and expectations. *Teacher* names a position whose incumbent may enact the roles of, for example, expert, coach, or evaluator. The teacher, for example, behaves as an expert lecturer when her students behave as uninformed listeners. (Were students to respond to her as informed talkers, the teacher's role-performance would shift accordingly.) Their histories and expectations incline students and teachers to enact those roles most likely to help them realize a desired return, we might say, from their interaction with each other. To encourage the return they wanted from Weber, his students enacted in writing for him those roles most likely to support a relationship with him that would lead to the outcome they wished from this course. Weber, similarly, designed and managed the journal assignment so as to support a desired relationship with his students and his superiors.

Analysis of individual journals shows their authors enacting varying roles in relation to their reader: their occupational, vocational, or familial roles, as well as their histories as students and writers, influenced their interpretation of their professor's roles and thus the ways they complemented (or didn't complement) them in their journals. In this chapter, I explore how their prior experiences as students and writers inclined two of my four informants, Beth and Tina, to negotiate the journal keeping so that it would support their goals for the course. I have chosen to focus on these two students because they are different from each other, and, together, representative of the range of students and writers in "Spaceship Earth." Beth was an older, nontraditional student, the same age as Weber. She had a wide range of writing experiences to draw on in keeping her journal, and a wider range of experiences in interacting with male authority figures at work and at school. Both her emotional maturity and her ambivalence about college and its roles and expectations set her in contrast to Tina, a more traditional undergraduate in her early twenties. Tina was a physics major from an academic family, well-versed in "essayist literacy" and comfortable in school and college, where she was used to doing well. The contrast between Beth's and Tina's use of the "Spaceship Earth" journal illustrates the interaction of personal psychology, academic and social history, and strategic rhetorical choice as students use journals to negotiate relationships with their teacher.

Beth: Goals for Journal Keeping in "Spaceship Earth"

Beth's conversations with me, her performance in class, and her journal entries suggest that, because she wanted credit for her journal, she attended carefully to Weber's expectations and to the roles he enacted in class. Doubting that her journal would satisfy her reader, she nonetheless wanted to validate her interpretation of the assignment. The time and energy required by Beth's outside-of-class obligations and her "discomfort" with academic writing meant that she produced what she called "disjointed" and "not thought out" journal entries. Although she knew Weber had said students could "think on paper" in their journals, Beth inferred from Weber's conduct of the class and his comments about periodical sources for entries that he preferred to read what he had also called "thoughtful reflections," and that he expected students to be using the library. Thus Beth doubted that the abrupt shifts in topic, the personal "gut reactions," and the lack of references to science magazines in her journal would work to develop her authority in Weber's eyes.

Wanting to present herself to her instructor as, in her words, "an intelligent thinking college student," but unwilling to substantially alter her "gut reaction" approach to journal keeping, Beth made compromises that are reflected in the rhetoric of her journal entries. To compensate for potential deficiencies in her thinking or writing, Beth expressed herself in her journal in the roles of uninformed, but appreciative, literate, and, we might say, dutiful student responding to an informed and respected teacher. She initially suppressed and later hedged reactions that might be inappropriate to this relationship. Although in her final entries, Beth felt encouraged to express herself in the previously suppressed roles of parent, joke teller, skeptic, and full-time worker, she did so in a manner befitting an appreciative student interacting with a teacher. Throughout the course, Beth filtered her expression of roles in which she felt most comfortable through the set she understood would win her professor's approval.

Beth's History as a Student and Writer: Learning a Rhetoric of Role Playing

Beth's experiences in communicating with teachers and employers and the particular circumstances of her work and school life in the summer of 1986 predisposed her to express herself as she did in negotiating Weber's assignment. Hampered by the demands of a full-time job and by lack of confidence in her power as an academic writer, Beth drew, in writing her journal entries, on the skills and abilities she had used to develop her authority as a parent, spouse, photographer, service industry worker, and professional cook, as well as college student. Beth's experiences in relationships with people who had more power than she—parents, teachers, employers, and a former spouse— inclined her to distrust stated intentions and motives. To help her win her parents' and teachers' attention (and later to manage her abusive spouse), Beth learned how to use roles in which she was comfortable in the service of relationships which called for her to express herself in roles with which she was not comfortable.

Talk—"the gift of gab," as she put it—was the most striking of Beth's means of developing rapport with others. Throughout her 43 years—most of them spent in rural northeastern Iowa—Beth had used her ear for others' language and her skill as a listener and storyteller to help her through tight spots with her children, co-workers, and teachers. Beth had learned as a schoolchild, however, that her love of talk (particularly mimicry) had to be controlled in her relationships with teachers. Her earliest school memory involved a kindergarten teacher making her "walk five times around the school building" because she had disrupted the class by "going to the pencil sharpener *too* many times in one morning."

"So," Beth told me, mimicking Mrs. Ulm's "singsongy" voice, "'Oh, Beth, she just wants to go for a walk, doesn't she,' so she grabbed my hand and paraded me around the room." From this episode, Beth had learned that although both she and her teacher were good mimics ("Bertha Ulm loved to talk, too"), Mrs. Ulm got to control the entertainment. (Until, as Beth concluded the story, "She had a stroke and never talked again. How about that?").

From Mrs. Ulm and other elementary teachers who embarrassed her for talking out of turn, mimicking others, and "mouthing off," Beth learned how teachers exercise their power to manage classroom discourse. Despite her frustration at having to "watch out" in school for verbal skills she was freer to exercise elsewhere, Beth was not inclined to challenge her teachers' power: "Most little farm girls don't rebel," she said. "Terrified" by her teachers, she expected them to take full advantage of their prerogatives to make the rules and implement them: "I like somebody that sets the rules. . . . If somebody is allowed to cheat in a class . . . I will lose respect for the teacher."

Beth also learned how teachers used what she called "bluffing" to manage their classes and develop the authority to which they were entitled. Most of the teachers she respected had underplayed or treated their erudition lightly, "not letting on how much they [knew]," she said. She felt she had learned the most from professors who demonstrated their "humanity" in class, and who used a sense of humor, enthusiasm, or eccentricity to make students interested in their material. (For example, a literature professor who "wore her galoshes rain or shine" and stored her library in a shopping cart captured Beth's respect with her extemporaneous recitations.) Beth sensed that Weber expressed an amiable, sometimes self-deprecating persona in class to encourage his students' trust and thereby develop his authority in their eyes. She asked me, during our first conversation, if I thought he had an "ulterior motive" for telling students to laugh at his jokes. Beth said that, like Weber, she found it useful to avoid "sounding arrogant":

If Weber thinks I'm smart, I'm going to let *him* think it. . . . I am smarter than my actions would lead one to think and I do that by choice. I think he does the same thing. He knows his subject and he does not have to go around trying to impress you with his knowledge. Because he knows what he's talking about, you know. That's kind of why I watch the journal. . . . I don't want to sound arrogant.

Not sounding arrogant in her journal entries came fairly easily to Beth partly because she lacked confidence in her ability to write (or "think") effectively for college professors. Her elementary and high school teachers had discouraged interest in critical literacy by emphasizing "neatness" in writing and teaching prescriptive grammar. An avid reader, Beth said she had enjoyed writing down "scraps" of dialogue and expressing her feelings in the diaries she kept sporadically. But outside of school, she had little use for the analytic or reflective prose expected of college students. Beth had achieved a high-*B* cumulative average as a college student, but she didn't seem to think it was likely she would use a university education to gain a professional career. As a part-time, "on again off again" student (at the sophomore level in the summer of 1986), Beth used college courses to help her express herself in the nonacademic roles—as, for example, wage-earner, parent, and amateur photographer—that she had pursued

since high school. (For example, "Spaceship Earth," in addition
to its academic benefits, gave Beth plenty of good conversation
material for her 2 1/2-hour round-trip commute to campus five
days a week with a companion enrolled in an "Iowa Geology"
course.)

Because her role as a college student, then, vied for her time
and attention with other equally important roles, Beth was
inclined to draw on her nonacademic talents in negotiating the
difficulties college assignments posed for her. Assigned in a university "Introduction to Radio Broadcasting" course, for example, to listen to six hours of radio programming for a minority
market and then write a "program profile," Beth used her ingenu-
ity as a raconteur to circumvent inconvenient procedural requirements. She told me the story of her program profile as
follows:

> Now I don't listen to radio, I don't have a radio, I can't stand
> it anyway, [but] I did try to find something. I called innu-
> merable stations for literature, got nothing. Got down to the
> deadline, so 24 hours before I had to have this [done]—I don't
> type either—I borrow this typewriter, got me some paper, I
> set down and I made up "Cooking With Inga." . . . I got that
> from—you know those stations that come in [here, Beth
> made the noise of radio static]—I caught a few words that
> she'd say—*delightful* woman. . . . You could just see it. She
> gave one recipe for Roquefort dressing and the rest of the
> time she talked about Mad King Ludwig's castle. Half an
> hour program, that's the only recipe she had. . . . Anyway I
> got an 85 percent and 95 was the best in the class. . . . I didn't
> lie in it. . . . I took something and made it into something.

Required in two of her college classes to keep journals, Beth had
similarly used her verbal and dramatic skills to help her compensate for her difficulties with these writing assignments.
Assigned in a "Psychology of Sleep and Dreams" course to record
her dreams in a journal, Beth "lost interest" in the journal keeping a couple of weeks into the course, and she stopped making
entries. (She told me she couldn't bring herself to expose to her
psychology professor the troubled content of her dreams and the
awkwardness of her unedited writing style.) Beth nonetheless
managed to earn an *A* for the course with her participation in
class and her term paper (an analysis of "lucid dreaming" that
made use of a book her professor had published on the subject).

In an American literature survey course, Beth had been assigned to keep a "double-entry reader-response journal." This proved more interesting for her than the dreams journal because she enjoyed reading novels and because the assignment was designed to encourage her to rethink the "gut reactions" she felt embarrassed to expose to a college professor. Although Beth was pleased with this journal, which she called her literature "photograph album," she compensated for any potential deficiencies in her writing or editing by winning her teacher's praise for her achievement with another assignment. (Beth singlehandedly scripted, produced, and directed a class dramatic production of *Uncle Tom's Cabin.*)

Beth's "Spaceship Earth" Journal: Negotiating Her Approach

With limited time and energy to write "Spaceship Earth" journal entries, and uncertain that her work would meet Weber's expectations, Beth drew on her nonacademic roles and abilities as well as her prior experience as a student to negotiate this journal assignment. In order to receive credit for entries that might be unacceptably short and "disjointed," that failed to make use of periodical sources, and that offered a point of view her professor might not share, Beth expressed herself in her journal as an appreciative and responsive student of Weber's material. She used her journal to develop rapport with Weber by complementing roles he expressed in class.

Responding to Weber's Expectations of Journal Entries Meeting Weber's expectation that journal keepers relate their own experiences of topics discussed in the course was not particularly difficult for Beth: as she put it in her June 18 entry, "I have been in a flood, tornado, a blizzard, a fire, a hail storm, a dust storm, a mock avalanche, and other [geological disturbances] and they have all had a very exhilerating (sp) effect upon my physical and mental person." As an amateur photographer (like her instructor), with a keen eye for design and an active imagination, Beth was ready to note, as she did in several of her entries, what Weber's slides, photos, and other illustrations of landforms reminded her of. Having lived for most of her life among people who farmed or supported farming for a livelihood—and interested in Weber's anecdotes about the mismanagement of resources—she was prepared to respond in kind with her own collection of "cases of pollution," reported in her June 27 entry.

> Just this week 3 cases of pollution have been discovered around the small town of [Taylor]. (1) a "large" farmer has been dumping his herbicides + pesticides in [Spring] Creek for over 10 years and this week one washed up into the park some one saw it and turned it in (2) the govt. man discovered a farm where the farmer was pumping hog waste directly into the ditch. It took 10 truckloads to pick it up and haul it away (3) a man disregarded the ban on Command and used it on his crops. When the plants all turned white, it too, was investigated and he will have to pay the price too. The point here is if there is this much pollution occurring within a nine mile radius in the heartland of Americia then the cumulative amount of pollution worldwide is staggering.

Alert and inquisitive as a student, but fearing that "too many" questions in class might lead Weber off the subject, Beth was also prepared to meet Weber's implicit expectation (indicated in the sample entries) that students raise questions in their journals. Beth asked one or two questions in almost every entry. She wondered, for example, about how wood becomes petrified (6/13), how suboceanic rifts can be photographed ("since . . . it is so dark that deep that light is unable to penetrate) (6/11), what caused the etched "overhangs" at a state park in her neighborhood (6/19), how the "fall" of a rock avalanche is calculated (6/19), why "geology persons" didn't predict subsidence under a university building (6/20), whether quicksand is a sinkhole (6/20), if "two huge boulders south of the field that I used to play on" are glacial deposits (6/23), why ceramic glazes harden as they do (6/25), how semiprecious metals are discovered (6/25), "how much copper by weight it took to make the skin of the Statue of Liberty" (6/26), whether a "cone of depression" is the reason that "when the barn water is on the house has no pressure" (6/26) and "what happens at the edge of space as we know it?" (7/2).

Justifying Her Interpretation of the Journal Assignment   Beth was prepared, then, to write what she told me were "off the cuff" entries that mentioned or raised questions about course-related topics with which she was familiar. She wasn't willing, however, to do any "research" as preparation for writing in her journal. Weber's assignment sheet had stated that "A good place to get inspirations for your journal is the periodicals section of the library. If you haven't been there, GO!!!" Nevertheless, Beth wasn't prepared to "hunt down geology articles." Her daily commute to campus and full-time job as a cook in a country club left her little time for homework. Typically, during the weekdays of the four-week summer session, Beth left for campus at 7:00 A.M., was in class from 10:00 until 2:30 P.M. (with an hour lunch break) and returned to her home town of Independence to work at the club from 4:00 P.M. until 2:00 A.M. She wasn't willing to make time for "research" in between classes, and she didn't have a convenient means of getting to campus on the weekends (when her fellow students typically made use of the library).

On June 20, Weber cited "good [periodical] sources" (such as *Science News*) for journal entries, reinforcing his assignment sheet directive that students use the library. Although Weber had not indicated that reactions to his expectations of journal keeping were appropriate material for entries, Beth was concerned enough that she might lose credit for failing to use "articles of research" that she justified her interpretation of the assignment in her June 20 entry. This entry begins: "My journal is not over articles of research because I understood the instruction sheet to instruct us to write as though we were thinking to ourselves so that's what I'm going to do." Worried that she was addressing an unsanctioned topic, Beth was careful to express herself here as a dutiful student: rather than indicating at this point (as she would in her final entry) that her outside-of-class roles and responsibilities prevented her from meeting the "sources" expectation, she chose instead to justify her "thinking to [her]self" in her writing on the grounds that she was simply doing what the assignment, as written, called for.

Beth nonetheless feared that if she failed to refer to current events she could potentially lose credit for her journal. Thus she immediately followed this defense of her approach with reference to an article in the campus newspaper: "I saw in the Northern Iowan today that housing is having problems with sinking." Later in the entry, Beth complained again about the journal assignment: "Don't like doing this journal. I have so many thoughts about the class lessons that I am frustrated in my attempts to put them down!"

When we discussed this entry, Beth told me that journal keeping was difficult for her, because she didn't have time to do it justice and because she was confused about what "Weber [was] looking for." Weber had given no indication that he would be likely to sympathize with the nonacademic constraints on Beth's time, or that he would appreciate hearing that she found his assignment confusing. Thus when she complained about the assignment in her journal, Beth offered reasons for disliking it that were appropriate to what she understood he would accept. That is, in writing that she didn't like doing the journal because she had "so many thoughts about the class lessons . . . !" she showed herself to be an enthusiastic student.

Two weeks later, when Weber asked students to "comment on the course" in their final entry, and when Beth had learned that Weber had held a full-time job when he was a college student, she complained that the journal was "a chore" because she didn't have time for it. She wrote that she "did not care to write the journal, it was a chore for me. As I drive a total of 2 1/2 hours a day, and work in Independence from 4 p.m. until 2 a.m. plus time in school I had precious little time to do it justice."

Having chatted with Weber during class breaks about her activities outside of class, Beth had reason to think he could appreciate the constraints a full-time job imposed on her. She had heard his request on July 1 that students "comment on" (evaluate) the course in their final journal entries. Lest she be construed as attacking the assignment, however, she followed the complaint quoted above with, "However, I believe [journal keeping] is a very good idea it forces you to think and that never hurts."

Compensating for "Not Enough" Beth typically wrote entries on her way to work, in the early hours of the morning after a ten-hour shift, or in the few minutes she had between obligations on campus. As luck would have it, a co-worker at the country club where Beth worked had taken "Spaceship Earth" the previous summer, and Beth said that she and this bartender often traded anecdotes about the class. Nonetheless, when she sat down to write in her journal after work, Beth said that she felt "talked out" (rather than inspired to write) by these conversations. The bartender, who had done well in the course, sometimes answered questions (about plate tectonics and flood stage measurement, for example) that Beth said she otherwise would have raised in her journal. These were reasons Beth told me that many of her entries were too short or, as she put it, "not enough for a full day."

On average, Beth's journal entries are not significantly longer or shorter than those produced by her fellow students (hers average three quarters of a page), but when she sensed they were insufficient, Beth softened her reader's potential irritation by expressing her appreciation for his material, or, as Weber often did, underplaying her grasp of it. On June 17, for example, Beth wrote:

> Given the uncertainty of earthquake predictions makes me wonder if the underlying causes of other natural occurrences are as accurate as we are led to believe. Maybe we are being subjected to educated guesses instead of a proposal based in fact. I am disturbed to discover all these things about volcanoes because I should have been inquistive (sp) enough before to find out on my own. That is one of the major things wrong with the population in general. We are content to sit back (for the most part) and let someone else do the work of hunting and searching. Status quo, let sleeping dogs lie, and if it doesn't concern you or yours directly let it alone. Wrong, wrong it's lazy. I did bad on the test. I got 3 and I know I have learned a whole lot more than that score would indicate. I had my old trouble of reading one thing and writing another. Strangely enough I am not too concerned with the grade I will get in this class because I will have learned an A's worth of information in any case. A person must be awed by them or at the very least impressed.

After a brief query about earthquake prediction, Beth expresses her appreciation for geology indirectly, denigrating her own potential as a geologist (and thereby conveying her need for Weber's expertise) by identifying herself with "the population in general," not "inquistive enough to find out on [its] own" and content to "sit back . . . and let someone else do the work." She then abruptly switches to an implied criticism of Weber's test, claiming that her grade fails to indicate how much she knows. Underplaying her own skill again, she blames the test problem partly on herself ("I had my old trouble of reading one thing and writing another"), and ends the entry by flattering Weber, claiming that she is unconcerned with her course grade because she "will have learned an A's worth of information in any case," and that the information is awesome (or at least impressive).

Negotiating an Acceptable Style Although Weber put in writing that he didn't care about grammar and spelling in the journal entries, Beth didn't "trust that . . . [because] nobody likes to read a lot of misspelled words." Because her spelling was "atrocious," writing without paying attention to it made her feel stupid . . . and [she] really resent[ed] that." Beth had several reasons for assuming Weber preferred "well-written" (free of surface error) text. His assignment sheet (which she read carefully) had asked for "thoughtful reflections." In her previous experience as a student, her teachers had for the most part conducted class and evaluated their students as Weber did, and they had always rewarded well-edited and proofread text. With the exception of his assigning students to keep journals, Weber appeared to Beth to be traditional in his expectations of students' work. Thus Beth felt "confused" about what Weber expected journal entries to look like, because she perceived a discrepancy between his urging students not to worry about spelling in their journals ("thinking on paper") and his expecting (more importantly) that, as college students, they should be able to produce literate text, or "thoughtful reflections."

To negotiate an acceptable compromise between these mixed signals, Beth said that "instead of taking the time to search for the right words, which many times . . . involves the dictionary," she chose "simplistic language" that she was "more apt to be able to spell." Although she didn't take the time to look up possibly misspelled words, she marked them with "sp" or "sp?" Over "rick-o-shay" in her June 19 entry she wrote, "I know this isn't spelled but sounded." She also did some rudimentary editing for clarity, moving infinitive phrases, replacing unclear personal pronouns (6/13), inserting missing articles (6/18) or phrases (6/19). She often inserted words in parentheses to clarify or elaborate: in her June 10 entry, for example, she wrote that "An interesting similarity, for me, is the medieval view about the universe and the view that children have that the world exists only in as much as they [have] knowledge of it." After "medieval view," she inserted the parenthetical "(ideas)" and, after "universe," she inserted "(world)."

Like the rhetoric of her June 26 entry, cited in the preceding section, these corrections and additions are points of compromise among competing interests that vied for Beth's attention as she wrote. Although Beth wanted to present herself as a literate writer and she didn't "want to be misinterpreted," she also didn't want to take the time to present her ideas in "properly . . . corrected" form. After all, for what it was worth, the assignment sheet had called for "thinking on paper."

But the "thoughtful reflections" expectation continued to worry Beth: she cut back her work hours on June 19 and took 20 minutes instead of the typical five or ten to write the next few entries. In her June 23 entry, longer by a half a page than preceding entries, she follows a "gut reaction" to her performance on the second test with a comment that "balance[s]" this reaction. The entry begins: "Going over the test right away, you get to kick yourself sooner." Beth then went on to write that the exam "also offered a unique opportunity for us to explore the errors in our comprehension of material to perhaps aid us in future endeavors." My questions for Beth about the shift in style between "kick[ing] [her]self sooner" and "exploring the errors . . . to aid us in future endeavors" suggested to her that her effort to "sound more like an adult . . . [hadn't] worked." During the next week, she spent no more time writing entries than she had spent the week before she resolved to "think through" her ideas more carefully. Only in her last two entries did she take the time (25 minutes) she needed to sustain focus on the ideas she addressed for more than two or three sentences. At this point in the course, she thought she needed to show her reader, before it was too late, what she was really capable of; she also guessed (correctly) that Weber would be likely to read first the entries containing the course evaluations he had asked for.

Negotiating a Point of View Some of the "many thoughts" Beth wanted to express in journal entries were philosophical: over the course of her 43 years, she had developed a consistent point of view about scientific constructions of the natural world and about human use of the environment. Like many of her fellow students, Beth, in her first entry, considered her "belief or non-belief" in the cosmological theory Weber had outlined and asked students to question on the first day of class. She was uncertain, at this point, whether Weber (a scientist) would share or accept her skepticism that the Big Bang—or any scientific theory—could explain human origins. Thus, in her first entry, Beth suppressed opinions she discussed with me, fearing that their "unscientific" nature could disconcert the reader for whom she didn't want to sound too "arrogant." Here is Beth's first entry, dated June 10:

> We have barely scratched the surface of the information available in this class and already I have a million questions forming in my mind. The "big bang" theory is a form of logic I cannot identify with at this stage. Maybe I will change my mind by the end of the four weeks when more supporting data has been absorbed. I really am to uninformed now to make a knowledge statement of my own belief or non-belief in the theory. The haunting questions

are 1. Where did the original mass come from? 2. If there is
an end to our universe what next? To imagine an infinite
nothingness staggers my mind.

When we discussed this entry, Beth told me that she believed
scientific theories of cosmology represent interpretations—scientists, she said, are "earth shapers." And so, for that matter, are
creationists: "I hear they took mind-altering drugs in the Bible,
so who knows?" Nonetheless she said she didn't buy the Big Bang
theory because "the God theory is just more comfortable to me."
Scientists posit a universe that she found uncomfortably amoral:
"I don't go to church, but . . . I don't want to come from a particle.
. . . I want to think God's up there." Although, in her journal
entry, Beth "wanted to say [about the Big Bang] . . . you prove it
and I still won't believe it," she chose not to because, she told me,
"that sounds like I'm arrogant and closed-minded." So she wrote,
"the big bang theory is a form of logic I cannot identify with at
this stage. Maybe I will change my mind by the end of the four
weeks when more supporting data has been absorbed." Her mind
did not change; but only three and a half weeks later, in her July
2 entry, did she develop her own position more fully:

Man can only rationalize, within his own frame of reference, his beginning and is sticking tenaciously to facts that
support his case. . . . It seems, to me, like scientist[s] (people
in general) try to make facts (data) support their ideas, accidently forget to mention those that contradict them and so it
goes . . . it is a very comforting feeling to believe one is here
because one is wanted and not because of some accident mil-
lions of miles away. Besides I still maintain until a satisfactory answer to basic questions like (1) where did the original
mass come from? and (2) nothing can be without an edge so
what happens at the edge of space as we know it?

Although Weber had said that there were unanswered questions about the Big Bang theory, Beth's position here challenges
an assumption (implicit in his remarks about constantly improving methodologies) that the truth of human origins may
someday be understood. Rather than pursuing an argument with
her reader, however, she followed the statement cited above with
an anecdote that concludes, "Dr. [Weber], how many things have
you mentioned over the years that have in someway altered,
forever, the thinking of another human being?" Praising Weber's

teaching in the anecdotal form Beth knew he liked, she hedged her preceding statement of a position that his teaching had not altered. In her final entry, discussed above, she similarly followed a complaint about the journal assignment with comments likely to assuage any ill-feeling.

Beth's strategies in negotiating the journal assignment reflect the fact that, in her experience, people typically could not be trusted to mean exactly what they said. Beth remembered the formative years of her life as a period during which she often felt humiliated and betrayed by people in positions of power over her. She had learned to express herself in a repertoire of roles that would win others' attention and approval. She owed much of her success as an adult—within and outside the university—to her skill at making use of her understanding that what people say is one of many cues to what they mean. In her "Spaceship Earth" journal, Beth's sensitivity to her reader's unstated expectations helped her develop and affirm the rapport she came to enjoy with him in class.

Because developing rapport with her teacher was, perhaps, more important to Beth than to many of her younger classmates, her strategies for ingratiating herself with him in her journal are more evident. Nonetheless, as Beth did, her classmates also used roles and abilities developed outside of class to negotiate an assignment described by Tina, to whom I turn next, as "open-ended." Although her goals for and approach to journal keeping differed from Beth's, Tina also drew on resources she had found effective as a writer and student in other contexts.

Tina's Goals for the Assignment

Like Beth's, Tina's strategies in negotiating the "open-ended" journal assignment represent compromises among her outside-of-class interests, her interest in doing well in the course, and her understanding of what her reader expected of journal keeping. As a student who expected to do well in the course—but who was uncertain how to prepare for Weber's exams—Tina used nine of her 18 entries as a "study guide" to "review . . . [and] reinforce" potential test material in Weber's lectures, the textbook, and the class nuclear energy debate. On the other hand, as a physics major accustomed to "challenging" herself, Tina was more inclined, especially after she found she had done well on the first test, to use her journal to pursue physics-related aspects of geology that she "hadn't [already] . . . learned about" (that is, taken notes on in class). In nine entries she summarized or otherwise made use of independent reading, specifically, Carl Sagan's *Cosmos* and various 1985 and 1986 issues of *Science News*.

As she summarized articles or reviewed course material, Tina drew on her experience explaining science topics in writing for her teachers. In order to learn from her writing, she was inclined to express herself "clearly"—to use what Scribner and Cole (1981) have called *essayist* strategies of development and coherence, for example. But because Tina understood that Weber wanted "thinking on paper," she didn't focus, organize, or edit her summaries as she would have if she were "turning [them] in for a grade." Like Beth, Tina wanted credit for her journal; she also wanted to "learn something . . . new from doing it." Her rhetoric represents the way Tina went about "learning something new" in the context of what she understood was expected of journal keeping. Tina's uses of her "Spaceship Earth" journal reflect her history as a successful student who had learned to use writing to develop her interest in science.

Tina's History: Using Writing to Learn about Science

People who mattered to Tina in her home, school, and work lives had encouraged and rewarded her interest in science and her ability to inform others about science in academic writing. In Tina's experience, home and school had always interconnected; she grew up in an Iowa college town and spent much of her early life in the company of adults who were involved in school-related or other professional careers. Tina's mother worked as a librarian at her elementary school, which was two blocks from their home. (Tina remembered that, when she came home for lunch as a grade schooler, she sometimes found one of her teachers there, visiting with her mother.) From her parents and her siblings (older than she by 11 and 15 years), Tina learned to read before she entered first grade. Inspired by books she checked out of the library, she wrote science fiction and "horse" stories in third grade. (She "wanted to be an astronomer or a veterinarian.") As she grew up, Tina's language, like her interests, reflected the kind of academic and professional literacy that surrounded her.

Describing her early experiences as a writer, Tina remembered using "adult" words like "astonishment" in a third grade paper: "Mom said, 'Are you sure you want to use that word; that's not a third grade word,' and I said, 'but Mom, I know what it means!'" By the time she graduated from high school, Tina had extensive practice not only in writing expository essays and term papers (she guessed she'd written "ten or 12"), but also in using writing to develop her growing interest in science, "the most challenging subject [she] could find." In a sophomore history class, for example, Tina effectively parlayed her interest in science into an assigned paper on World War Two. Tina said this about the assignment:

> I thought, "I don't really want to know . . . about World War Two, but I like science," so I was going to incorporate the two. . . . I wrote it on the atom bomb, all about how it works and everything. . . . It was a science paper really [but] . . . I got an A+ on it.

Tina guessed that, of the "three or four" term papers she wrote each semester in high school, at least one dealt with a science topic. In a "College Prep Composition and Rhetoric" class, for example, her response to a "letter to the editor" assignment was "An Ecological Disaster" (an argument against draining run-off ponds in a marshland community); her "essay on a literary work" was "*On Walden Pond*"; and her "research paper" was "Three Cosmological Models."

Although writing papers that satisfied her was "a struggle" for Tina, her experience explaining science topics in writing for her elementary and high school teachers prepared her for the writing assignments she negotiated successfully as a university physics major. By the time Tina had reached junior standing in 1986 (when she was 20 years old), she had written "a couple dozen" lab reports in her courses in general and solid state physics, mechanics and quantum mechanics, astronomy, holography, and electronics.

Tina was inclined, then, to "learn the most," as she put it, from writing in which she expressed herself to her readers as her teachers and the authors of books she enjoyed had expressed themselves to her. That is, she preferred writing to inform her readers, educating herself in the process. If Tina's term paper writing and lab reporting experiences had taught her how to represent and document reported information effectively, her experiences keeping journals in and outside of school suggested (indirectly) that her strongest incentives to write stemmed from the conviction she was informing somebody of "something [she did]n't know about . . . something new." That hadn't happened in the two journal keeping experiences she described, and both times the writing had been difficult for her.

Tina had tried, dutifully, to fill in spaces in a five-year diary her parents had given her for Christmas when she was in seventh grade. Not long after starting, she had abandoned the effort:

> "This is stupid," I thought, "What could possibly be important about what I had to say?" . . . Since then I've thought, "Boy I wish I'd kept that diary because it was really neat how I thought back then. . . . Maybe I would have liked it better if it was just, you know, [undated] pages but . . . given a certain space for each date, I thought, "Well I have to do it *every* day and I don't want to!" . . . I think I only kept [that diary] . . . for a week or so.

Tina also remembered as "frustrating" her experience keeping a journal in an introductory college physics class (used the following year as a site for a study of journal keeping—Jensen, reported in Fulwiler, 1987). Journal keepers in this class were assigned, Tina said, to "pretend that we were . . . explaining to other people [a roommate or a younger brother, for example] some principle [her professor] went over." The assignment had called for "basically spouting back what we learned in class." Although Tina was frustrated that she lacked leeway to pursue her own interests, she turned in the required number of entries and received full credit for them. Her experience summarizing her instructor's material in a science class journal may have inclined her to take a similar approach (that is, to write summaries) in her "open-ended" "Spaceship Earth" journal.

In the summer of 1986, Tina was well on her way to successful completion of the physics major, and she needed to take one more of the required university general education courses. She enrolled in "Spaceship Earth" because "it was the only one that looked remotely interesting." In negotiating the journal assignment, Tina drew on her experience at making her teachers' expectations a kind of frame, we might say, in which she could pursue her own interests in science.

Tina's "Spaceship Earth" Journal:
Negotiating a Useful and "Suitable" Approach.

"Unsure" of what Weber was looking for, Tina initially took her cue from the sample entries: she took as a title for her first entry ("Lecture on: Gross structure of the universe") one of the sample titles. Like the authors of the samples and many of her classmates, Tina commented on class activities or textbook material in four of her first week's entries. Disinclined, however, to "spout back" Weber's or the textbook material, Tina chose to alter her approach when she no longer needed her journal as a "study guide." In her *Science News* summaries, she reported on current events more closely related to her physics interests than what Weber presented in class. She did so, however, with an eye to their "suitability," as journal material, and she represented what she reported with the intent to "explain [herself] clearly" to her readers.

Reviewing Potential Test Material Tina, like many of her classmates, was "uncertain" about how to study or what to prepare for Weber's exams. Rather than outlining or rewriting class notes (or shifting, as Beth did, from unelaborated point to point), Tina characteristically sustained concentration on one or two topics throughout each roughly one-page entry, following a new term or concept with an explanation, or a question with an answer. After reporting, for example, in her June 18 entry, that she had learned about "quick clays" in Chapter 9 of the text, she went on to define and explain them:

> I just read Chapter 9 on mass movement. One interesting tidbit I learned is about something called "quick clays." Weathering of volcanic ash or the grinding and crunching action of glaciers can produce *very* fine grains of particles called rock flour. If this material comes in contact with sea water the salt will, when the material is uplifted out of the ocean, act as a "glue" and these clay-sized particles will stick together after the seawater evaporates. Subsequent introduction of fresh water dissolves and washes away the salt, leaving behind a very porous and delicately connected "rock." Seismic waves can then break these fine structures and the resulting material is very prone to sliding.

Tina's paragraph on quick clays hews closely to the section entitled "Quick Clays" in the textbook; the information she includes
and its sequencing are almost identical, though the wording
is not. Here is the relevant textbook passage (Montgomery 1986,
p. 156):

> True *quick clays* are most common in northern latitudes.
> The grinding and pulverizing action of massive glaciers can
> produce a *rock flour* of clay-sized particles, less than .02
> millimeter (.0008 inch) in diameter. When this extremely
> fine material is deposited in a marine environment, and the
> sediment later uplifted above sea level by tectonic move-
> ments, it contains salty pore water. The sodium chloride in
> the pore water acts as a glue holding the clay particles
> together. Fresh water subsequently infiltrating the clay
> washes out the salts, leaving a delicate honeycomb-like
> structure of particles not firmly held together. Vibration
> from seismic waves breaks the structure apart, reducing the
> strength of the quick clay by as much as 20 to 30 times, cre-
> ating a finer-grained equivalent of quicksand which is
> highly prone to sliding.

Subsequent journal entries took the same form. After asking,
in her June 10 entry, "What exactly is a quasar?" or, in her June
12 entry, "What causes volcanoes to erupt?" Tina provided answers that, she said, "paraphrased" her notes and reading. She
used five of her first six entries to "review . . . [and] reinforce"
material with which she was least familiar: for example, the
"most dangerous outcomes" of volcanic activity (not lava, but
noxious gases and ash) (6/14); and "long term after effects of
earthquakes" (6/18). After establishing class topics or her reading as the context for writing ("Today we learned about seismic
waves," [6/18], "We went over the test today" [6/16], or "I just read
Chapter 9 on mass movement" [6/18]), Tina characteristically
pursued a point of interest—a "detail" (6/10) or a "tidbit" (6/18)—
that Weber had not discussed.

A few days after the first exam, however, Tina lost her incentive to continue summarizing lecture and textbook material in
her journal. Although she expected to do as well on Weber's second and third exams as she had on the first, she began to find it
"repetitious" to use her journal to review material she could
grasp adequately from reading her text or taking notes in class.

She preferred to report on "new" information, in the context of what she understood was appropriate to the assignment.

Making Appropriate Use of Science Interests   Tina's background and interest in physics topics—especially cosmology and seismology—appear throughout her journal. Her first entry, for example, unlike those of any of her classmates, concludes with speculation about cosmological principles that had not been part of Weber's review of the subject. Nonetheless, Tina pursued her own science interests with an eye to what she understood was appropriate to journal keeping as Weber assigned it. Accepting that the topics she addressed should be relevant to course material, for example, she chose not to follow up on what she understood to be the physics questions that she had raised in her fifth entry, dated June 17. Tina's understanding of basic fluid dynamics had prompted her to raise questions about the names and behaviors of earthquake waves that Weber had defined in class. In her journal, she asked: "Why can s-waves only travel through solids? Other kinds of transverse waves can travel through liquids. . . . How are all of these waves connected? . . . *Are* they? Why are there 3 different types?"

After asking these questions in her journal, Tina had spent some time in the library looking for answers, but she decided not to report on what she had discovered. "This a physics [and not a geology] problem," she said. So she decided "not to take the time to go into" it:

> I looked in a couple of [geology] books about the s-waves in the library. . . . They just said notice that s-waves do not go through the molten core. That's all they say. They don't say why, either. . . . It's got to be much more complicated than just transverse and longitude. . . . Fluid dynamics might be able to tell more why. . . . It's something to think about [but] I didn't really want to take the time to go into it. . . . Maybe it's something I'd ask . . . in a physics class, if it came up.

Tina also chose not to "go into" her fluid dynamics questions because she guessed that Weber was not likely to read or respond to them. When I asked Tina on July 3 how seriously she had taken Weber's assignment sheet comment that "from time to time [he might] collect and read the journals," Tina answered:

I never expected him to [read the journals]. Especially for four weeks, I thought, "Come on, you got to be kidding." There's never enough time for them to read things like this. Maybe some of them do, but not in this type of class.

Tina's entry of June 17 was the last in which she raised any questions. Instead, in six of her next nine entries, she summarized short (500–750-word) features she read in 1985 and 1986 issues of *Science News*, a "general interest . . . semitechnical" weekly magazine. She was interested in current events in science, and Weber had advised students to consult outside sources of information. Having "thought about" using the back issues from her expired subscription to *Science News* (conveniently "lying around the house"), Tina chose to do so on June 20. Weber had come to class that day with a copy of *Science* that he held up as an example of a "good source" for journal entries. Tina volunteered *Science News* as "another good one." Then, after class, she caught up her journal by writing two entries (the first dated June 19) that summarized "suitable" articles.

Choosing Suitable Material Tina sensed that summaries would not exactly match her instructor's expectation that "inspirations" for entries could come from science periodicals. She pointed to her first, longest, and most reflective entry as "what a journal should be." Here, she had used outside reading (Sagan's *Cosmos*) to supplement her own questions and speculations. (Several weeks later, Weber concurred with this assessment, saying that summaries of students' reading were "not really what [he] wanted to see.") But since the physics-related questions Tina had raised in her first and other entries were going unanswered, and since Weber had approved in class of her information source, if not her approach to it, Tina decided she would "learn more" by summarizing *Science News* features than by raising questions or reviewing course material. Tina never doubted Weber would accept and give credit for her journal, in part because she was careful to choose "suitable" articles to summarize.

"Suitability" represented a compromise among Tina's interests (particularly in the physics of earthquakes) and her understanding of appropriate topics and the appropriate length for a "Spaceship Earth" journal entry. As she looked through her magazines, she had been interested, she said, in a "long" (perhaps 5,000-word) feature on the behavior of quasars, but she rejected this as summary material on the grounds that it was "too long" and "not enough to do with geology." Tina's previous experience as a journal keeper, and the sample entries Weber had projected, had suggested that entries should be "a little bit [of thought] . . . maybe a page or so." Her process in choosing suitable summary material reflects her length and topic expectations:

[To] find a suitable article . . . I tried to stay away from the main articles [which were] too long and involved to write on in one page. Some of them had no connection to anything we had done in class. So, I had to read a couple of those before I decided, well, I'd better not do this. [Then] I'd read some short ones—maybe seventy five, a hundred words—but some of them just didn't have anything of substance in them. So I had to find a suitable article, which was usually the short [500–750-word current events] features.

All her remaining entries, from June 19 onward, except those on essentially assigned topics (the in-class writing on the light bulb, debate preparation, and the final "comment on the course" entry) Tina devoted to summaries of *Science News* features titled "Making a Date with Light," "A Fault of Youth," "Alaskan Great Quake: Ready or Not?", "Damage in Mexico: A Double Quake," "When the Earth Quakes the Sand Blows," and "When Forcing Fluids Makes Quakes." Tina found these articles suitable because they all reported events that were "connected" in one way or another with Weber's discussions of geologic dating and earthquakes; they were all short enough to be summarized in one page, but long enough to have "substance"; and they all offered Tina new information on topics that interested her.

Exercising Her Knowledge of Physics   As she looked for "suitable" articles to summarize, Tina was drawn to those that her "knowledge of physics helped [her] . . . understand and explain." She was particularly interested in developments in seismology—in how earthquake waves work. This interest is evident, for example, in the way Tina chose to represent an article called "Damage in Mexico: A Double Quake," taken from the January 11, 1986 issue of *Science News*. The article reads as follows.

Damage in Mexico: A double quake

The big question nagging seismologists and engineers since the Sept. 19 earthquake devastated sections of Mexico

City and killed almost 10,000 people (SN: 9/28/85, p. 196) has been why this quake caused so much damage. One factor is that the ground-shaking was amplified—scientists now say by about five times—because Mexico City lies on an old lake bed that resonates with the seismic waves. The thickness of the bed is such that the seismic waves that are the most amplified are the low-frequency signals, which can do the most damage to taller buildings. Other notable quakes may not have been as devastating, scientists say, because there were not as many tall buildings in the past.

But recently, seismologists have come to think that the deadliness of the Sept. 19 quake was also due in part to its long duration. In fact, the main shock of the magnitude 8.1 quake was really a double event, consisting of two 16-second tremors spaced about 26 seconds apart. The rupture started in the northwest part of the Michoacan gap—a segment of the Mexican subduction zone (where the Cocos oceanic plate is plunging beneath the North American plate) that had been tagged as a likely place for an earthquake. The second tremor was triggered by the first, 90 kilometers to the southeast. According to James Beck at Caltech in Pasadena, Calif., the unusually long period of shaking allowed more time for the lake bed to amplify ground motion and made some buildings more flexible so that they resonated more easily with the low-frequency seismic waves. Beck notes that the building codes in Mexico City had taken into account the effect of low-frequency waves, but Jorge Prince of the National Autonomous University of Mexico adds that none of these codes had specified the number of cycles of shaking that a building should withstand.

Seismologists say the Sept. 19 earthquake is one of the best-documented quakes in history. "This is the first time we can make a good comparison between the source region of such a big earthquake and the energy radiated out to large distances," observes James Brune at Caltech. With strong motion instruments, Brune and his co-workers found that ground motion near the fault was actually quite low, about 15 percent of the acceleration due to gravity (g). In comparison, the ground motion near California faults can reach values six to seven times that. Brune says the acceleration, which had dropped to about 4 percent g outside of Mexico City, was boosted to about 20 percent g inside the city. While scientists had known that the lake bed would resonate, they had little idea of what the amplification would be, he adds.

Because the Mexico earthquake had little or no precursory signals, Brune thinks seismologists should concentrate on ground-motion monitoring so that engineers designing buildings know what to expect when an earthquake does come. And now that the Michoacan gap has ruptured, all eyes are turned to the Guerrero gap to the south, which has been ominously quiet since 1911.[1]

Tina summarized the article in her June 24 entry, as follows:

An article called "Damage in Mexico: A double quake" appeared in the January 11, 1986 issue of *Science News*.

There was much more damage in the Sept. 19, 1985 Mexico City earthquake than the scientists would have predicted. They think one of the factors involved is the fact that Mexico City is on an old lake bed that resonates with the seismic waves and, thus, amplifies them. The lake bed's thickness is such that the low frequency signals are the ones that are amplified the most, and it is these low frequency signals that do the most damage to tall buildings.

Another reason for the severity of this earthquake was its long duration. There were two 96 sec. tremors, about 26 seconds apart measuring 8.1 on the Richter Scale. This unusually long tremor allowed the lake bed enough time to really amplify the ground motion.

The building code in Mexico City had taken into account the effect of the low frequency waves, but not the duration of these—in other words the buildings might have withstood a few seconds of shaking but not the length of this unusually long earthquake.

The effect of the lake bed resonance was such that near the fault itself the ground motion was about 15% of acceleration due to gravity (g); then it fell to about 4% g outside the city. Inside the city itself under which the lakebed set, however; the ground motion had risen to 20% of the acceleration due to gravity.

---

[1] Reprinted with permission from *SCIENCE NEWS*, the weekly news magazine of science. Copyright © 1986 by Science Service, Inc.

The approximately 750-word *Science News* feature reports findings that the September 19, 1985 Mexico earthquakes were unexpectedly severe; Mexico City, as Tina put it, "lies on an old lake bed that resonates with the seismic waves and, thus, amplifies them." After providing information about the duration, intensity, and other effects of the "double quake," the (unidentified) authors of the feature conclude that building engineers should do more "ground motion monitoring." Rather than making this her conclusion, Tina gave the last paragraph of her (approximately 240-word) summary to technical information about the intensity of the ground motion under the "double quakes." As an experienced reporter of science topics, Tina had been careful to represent the gist of the article in layman's terms and in the first paragraph, where a reader would expect to find it. She wrote the summaries, she said, "to explain [their topics] to [her] readers." Nonetheless, her own background and interest in physics inclined her to give about a quarter of her summary to technical information that had comprised less than a fifth of the original.

Although interested in exercising her physics knowledge and using writing to learn about and explain the subjects she reported on, Tina wasn't willing to go to the trouble in doing so that she might have, were she "turning [entries] in for a grade." Although, for example, her summary of "Damage in Mexico" included technical information about acceleration due to gravity (g), she hadn't chosen to find out exactly what that meant, doubting that it would "matter too much" to her readers. When I asked her how acceleration due to gravity worked, she responded:

> Acceleration due to gravity. Well . . . it's fifteen percent of some constant. So, it's 15 percent of 9.8 meters per second squared. So that's some acceleration—what, acceleration of the ground motion or—the only thing I can think of—the ground motion was changing more rapidly at one point than at another point, I guess. I think that's what they're saying. I had not really quite seen g's in that context—the ground motion in terms of g. I'm not really certain what they were talking about. I didn't think it would matter too much.

As a student of physics, Tina had chosen to incorporate technical information in her summary; as a "Spaceship Earth" journal keeper, she had left that information undigested, we might say: her interest had stopped at figuring out and trying to explain it. After all, her reader would not be likely to care.

Negotiating a Workable Style Like Beth's, Tina's style in writing—the structure and language of her entries—represent compromises, in this case between her sense of her reader's expectations and her goals as a science student who wanted to learn from and inform others in her writing. Unlike Beth, Tina accepted that Weber wanted "thinking on paper," or, as she put it, "a little bit of thought." Although her writing style was "not what it could be," Tina "wasn't going to worry about it." Of her first entry, Tina said this:

> I was thinking, "This is really bad grammar. . . . Boy, I could have worded that better. . . . I should have had two sentences there instead of one. . . . But I was continuing cause he said, "It doesn't matter; you shouldn't worry about it." So I thought, "I'm not going to worry about it!"

Thus Tina left uncorrected the "volcanoes" she recognized as misspelled (in her 6/12 entry), and "didn't bother" to add a missing *ly* to an adverbial "actual." She neither edited nor planned her journal entries as she said she would if each entry were to be graded. This meant that she "sometimes just threw in" transitional connectives; referring to her June 20 entry, Tina said, "I have a 'first' but no 'second.'" And "rather than try to incorporate what should have come earlier" in her June 16 entry, Tina appended a "footnote" (i.e., "if you measured the height of mountains from the sea floor Hawaii would be the highest mountain in the world").

Nonetheless, Tina used in her journal cues to organization like "footnote," coherence devices like "for example" or "another reason," explanatory modification like "white holes (the other side of black holes)" or "photons (light)," transitional connectives like "first," "finally," "therefore," and "hence," and she focused on one topic per paragraph in entries with a typically introduction–body–conclusion structure. These "essayist" patterns in her style suggest that Tina's training in meeting academic readers' expectations came into play as she negotiated a style that would encourage her to learn and inform even as she engaged in only "a little bit" of thought. She described her process in writing *Science News* summaries this way:

> I read the article and . . . thought, "Well, what is it . . . trying to say—if you just [copy] it, you're not really learning that." So I wanted to make sure I understood the content. I was

thinking . . . if I was going to explain it to [my readers] what
would I need to put in there. So I drew on my knowledge of
physics to rephrase it.

Tina's experience as a writer of expository prose, as well as her
knowledge of physics, are reflected in the way she organized and
edited her summaries with an academic but nonspecialist reader
in mind. In an article in her June 20 entry, Tina summarized a
short feature, "Making a Date with Light," that is written for a
reader who has some background in physics. Tina first named
and dated the article, and she explained, as did her source, why
the new technique is needed. Then, departing from the rhetoric of
her source, Tina offered "First, some background information"
about how the effects of radioactivity on crystal structure make
laser dating possible. The article provides this information, but
Tina cued the reader to its relevance and paraphrased it in somewhat less technical language. Here is the second paragraph of
"Making a Date with Light":

> [This] technique is based on the ability of radiation, pro-
> duced in the decay of naturally occurring isotopes, to ionize
> electrons from atoms in the mineral crystal. These elec-
> trons then fall into traps or defects in the crystal. . . . the
> number of captured electrons is, therefore, a measure of the
> time elapsed since the last exposure to light, and presumably
> the deposition age of the sediment.

And here is the second paragraph of Tina's summary:

> First, some background information: minerals are crys-
> talline in structure, but they are not perfect crystals, i.e.
> there are defects or holes in this regular array of molecules.
> Naturally occurring radioactivity can ionize electrons in
> the atoms that form the crystalline structure, and those
> freed electrons fall into the "holes" in the crystal. When
> these electrons are exposed to light (photons) they can escape
> these holes.

Tina's interest in writing accurately as well as clearly is also
evident in her editing of her summary of "Damage in Mexico: A
Double Quake." This article reports that "The big question nagging seismologists and engineers since the Sept. 19 earthquake
devastated sections of Mexico City and killed almost 10,000 peo-

ple . . . has been why this quake caused so much damage." Then, in its second paragraph, the article identifies its thesis: "But recently, seismologists have come to think that the deadliness of the Sept. 19 quake was also due in part to its long duration." After naming and dating the article, Tina wrote: "There was much more damage in the Sept. 19, 1985 Mexico City earthquake than the scientists first th." Then she crossed out "first th" and replaced it with "would have predicted." She explained the change this way:

> I thought, "Well, . . . [the article] isn't saying that ["first thought]." The earthquakes happened and they got data. Then a little while later, they got better data, and . . . it did more damage than they thought at first. Before that, they wouldn't have figured this much damage would have occurred. So there's a difference there.

Although Tina and Beth used similar strategies in negotiating the journal assignment—both found workable compromises among their interests and their perceptions of their reader's interests—Tina wrote with considerably more confidence that her approach would be acceptable. Her teachers had almost always liked and encouraged her work. Tina had excelled as a student not only because she could do scientific calculations very well *and* write very well; in learning to write and calculate, she had also, meanwhile, internalized her teachers' expectations of her performance so successfully that she could accurately interpret and easily produce what they were looking for in her work. Beth was also skilled at assessing her teachers' implicit agendas. A difference between them was that Tina would not have described herself as an interpreter of what Beth called "ulterior motives"; Tina assumed that she was doing what was expected. At age 20, with 14 years of schooling behind her, Tina was an academic insider, we might say; she lacked Beth's outsider's perspective. For Beth, at age 43 and with many years of experience in other kinds of institutions besides school, academia was a place for learning, but it was simultaneously a social and political institution like any other. It was clear to Beth, but not to Tina, I think, that doing well in college didn't just mean writing, reading, calculating, and "thinking" well, it also meant knowing how to read and play the politics of schooling.

5

THE SOCIOPOLITICS
OF JOURNAL KEEPING
IN "SPACESHIP EARTH":
THE PROFESSOR

I turn now to Carl Weber, the instructor of "Spaceship Earth." In what follows, I trace how Weber's history as a teacher and as a writer shaped his understanding of writing in general, and journal keeping in particular. I describe what he hoped "Spaceship Earth" would accomplish, what he expected from the journal assignment, and how he evaluated his students' efforts. The influence of academic politics on a teacher's ideology and pedagogy is a central theme in the sequence of events that led Weber to assign and use journals as he did in the summer of 1986, and it is also a theme of this chapter.

Assigning Writing in "Spaceship Earth"

Carl Weber's assignment of a journal in "Spaceship Earth" reflected his competing interests as an educator, as the teacher of this particular course, and as a professional academic. Carl was deeply committed to teaching, having left a job as a state geologist to return to school for his doctorate because he thought he could "spend [his] life productively in society better by teaching." He was convinced that although "teaching may be banging one's head somewhat . . . one gets through occasionally, and [in teaching] you have an ability to have a greater impact far into the future and a lasting impact." Carl had general, introductory courses like "Spaceship Earth" specifically in mind as his teaching mission: "'Spaceship Earth' was the kind of course [in which he] could make [his] greatest impact."

As an educator, Carl had learned from his teaching and writing experiences—many of them outside academia—that writing is "an excellent way to think," and that the production of written text is an "evolving" and "collaborative" process. In upper level geology courses, he had had great success with collaborative writing projects designed to prepare students for what they would be likely to do as professional geologists. In 1985, for example, he had 18 students in an environmental geology course act as if they were the staff of the local branch office of a company called Landfill Services, reporting to the home office on the best local site for a hazardous waste dump. The students were required to produce a formal written report and present it orally to an invited audience. The group had to "work as a team," even when the person playing the role of project manager proved unequal to the job. Carl "wanted them to have some of the frustrations of this kind of an experience." He "wanted them to have to go out and have to use their brains, their imaginations on how to solve some of the problems," and he saw a joint writing project as a good way to encourage this. Though some students found the project frustrating, Carl sensed that "the ones that were a little more mature recognized the value they were getting out of it."

In his first few years of teaching "Spaceship Earth," Carl implemented his ideas about the importance of writing in an ambitious student writing agenda that included submission of rough and final drafts of a required "article critique" and participation in a peer review of critique drafts, as well as journal keeping and essay exams. Though "they have always been unpopular," essay tests told Carl "more about the students . . . more about what the students could be learning." However, the extensive course syllabus Carl inherited was not designed to accommodate much student-initiated activity in the form of talk or writing, and Carl, a nontenured assistant professor, was not inclined to radically alter the structure or the expected teaching methods—the "lecture style format"—of this high enrollment general education course. Committed, nonetheless, to "mak[ing] writing practice more a part of undergraduate education," Carl assigned his "Spaceship

Earth" students considerably more writing than they typically encountered in general education courses.

In the first 2 1/2 years that Carl taught the course (each fall, spring, and summer session from fall 1982 through spring 1985), students complained about his writing assignments in semester evaluations that Carl's promotion advisory committee regarded as evidence of unsatisfactory teaching performance. Carl "got strong signals," he said, that "bringing up"—raising the point totals—of the primarily quantitative evaluations was prerequisite to his receiving tenure.

To maintain his commitment to providing "meaningful" writing practice for students whose resistance to his efforts to do so could evidently jeopardize his career, Carl considered several possible options. Since he alone taught "Spaceship Earth," any curricular changes were his to initiate. One option was to renegotiate the course agenda so that writing could somehow be better integrated in class activity. Carl had "always thought," he said, that "we ought to talk more about the journals [and papers] . . . in class. We ought to be doing more with them." If students got more and faster responses to their writing and if their journals, peer review session, and article critique could be as important to their final grade as their grasp of lecture and textbook material, perhaps the writing assignments would be better received. This option would require change in the content of the course: Carl realized that he "couldn't cover as much material if [students] spent much more time writing [or using writing as impetus to discussion] in class." This option would also require change in the way the course was taught: more time for student writing and talk in class would leave less for lecturing. But class discussion would be unwieldy, if not infeasible, in a course that, during the fall and spring semesters, enrolled 50 to 75 students in each of the two sections Carl taught.

There was a further curricular reason to leave the course as it was. Given the roles that Carl's predecessors had assigned "Spaceship Earth" in both the earth science department's program of offerings and in the interdepartmental curricular program of general education, its broad survey goals and lecture mode of instruction were understood to be essentially nonnegotiable. It would take a heroic amount of time, energy, and lobbying for an untenured instructor in Carl's position to revamp the course. Even though plans to revise the university's general education program were underway in the spring of 1985, and Carl was a member of the committee charged with overseeing them, he decided it "wasn't worth it" to change a course that might be replaced altogether.

An easier and more expedient option was simply to drop the offending writing assignments from the "Spaceship Earth" syllabus. Within a year of teaching the course, Carl was finding that the task of reading boxfuls of journals and grading scores of poorly written papers each semester was tedious, at best. As he put it, "If you assign [term papers], you have to really read and really comment on everything. That became unbearable. . . . [T]he last time I did this I literally sprained my back sitting there in a position, reading them." In the spring of 1985 he began to have "serious doubts" about the worth of requiring critical writing of students who were, typically, neither prepared for nor expecting assignments like his. He was "always frustrated" with the critical analysis papers he received; he "wanted the students to take an article . . . analyze that and think critically . . . [about] the ideas presented in that paper," but found that "in some cases, [the student] didn't even know what the paper was about . . . couldn't even read the paper and understand what it was saying," or "didn't have enough understanding of the topic outside of that article [so] that they had anything to compare to." Since UNI had neither a freshman writing requirement nor a formal program of writing emphasis courses in the upper division, Carl's approach was, by and large, unsupported in the rest of the curriculum. In a 1984 writing-across-the-curriculum newsletter article in which he described and advocated his writing assignments, Carl complained that "the lack of required writing courses simply cannot be compensated for in other courses" ([Weber], 1984).

In the spring semester of 1986 (after hearing from his promotion committee), Carl did not require an article critique or a journal of his "Spaceship Earth" students, and he replaced the essay exams with multiple choice. Reluctant to make these changes, he found them unsatisfactory: it was difficult to teach students who "were [not] doing . . . any thinking outside of class." They responded to him in class "like bumps on a log."

Restoring the journal assignment and handling it as he did in the summer of 1986 appeared to be a workable compromise among his interests in teaching a course that was not designed to incorporate writing assignments, providing resistant students with pedagogically defensible writing practice, and, meanwhile, protecting his career. Carl's history as a writer and teacher suggests that assigning his students to keep journals helped him put his ideology as an educator in practice, while it also helped him manage his classes comfortably and respond to institutional expectations of his performance.

Carl's Expectations for the Journals: Making Connections

The ideal student journal, to Carl's mind, was one in which the writer made connections between "Spaceship Earth" material and everyday, real-world experience. Having students make connections of this sort was a key goal of the course, which Carl taught in such a way as "to emphasize the interaction between earth processes and materials and human activities and human concerns." He wanted students to "make the connection that, by gosh, this earth we are living on with these processes and these materials . . . [has] a lot to do with who we are, what we are, and what we are doing here on this planet." He hoped that journal writers would "take a jump" to "integrate" the subject material with their lives.

Carl's oral evaluations of the "Spaceship Earth" journals, in conversation with me, reflected this concern. This means that many of the uses to which students put their journals (discussed in Chapter 3) were not what their instructor had in mind. Of one of the many journals in which the writer rewrote and summarized class notes, Carl said, "[this sort of entry] is good in the sense that it probably helps [the student] learn about what you talked about in class, but the jump to making it [her] own isn't necessarily there." He wanted students to "think about [the material] a little bit in their own words, their own kind of thinking," and he liked the early entries in Tina's journal in which he saw her doing that. To Tina's journal entry question, "I've never really thought about, where all the planets come from? or came from?" Carl's response was, "she's thinking about something new and it's good." Tina's later *Science News* summaries were "not really what [Weber] wanted," since "she [was] simply reporting on [the articles] and not giving it much of her own thought." He liked entries that began with, "I never really thought about the elements or where they came from," or included statements like, "Boy, did I learn a lot." "If you can only get a person to do that a couple times a semester," he said, "you've accomplished something."

Carl believed that effective journal entries should not be written with himself as the explicit audience. For this reason, he liked Beth's referring to him in the third person, which showed, he said, that "she is not writing this to me, which is good." Knowing from his own experience that writing for a professor who "knows so much more" puts students "in a bind," Carl wanted students to envision their own audience, "figure it out and come up with their own answer." And although he was interested in comments about his teaching style (and regularly read the last, course-evaluation entry first when journals were handed in), he felt that this was not a good use of the journals, either, and objected to Beth's "Dr. [Weber] used copper as an example of a resource base" and other commentary about him as being "not the intention of the journal."

His view of journal writing as personal and self-expressive led Carl to a principled decision not to make written comments on journals when they were handed in at the term's end. Though "very occasionally" providing written commentary, Carl thought that "any comment [he] would make could be interpreted . . . as being judgmental" and inappropriate, since he told students that journals would not be graded. Although Carl "react[ed] rather strongly sometimes in [his] gut to what [he] read in those journals," expression of his personal reaction was also, he thought, inappropriate. Providing his "opinions on their opinions" would be contrary to the goals of general education courses, which are, he said, "to get [students] to think and come to their conclusions, not the conclusions that [the teachers] have already drawn" or the teachers' "particular set of emotions and values." There was also a more practical reason for not commenting on journals: few students ever came by after the semester's end to pick them up. Journals counted in Carl's grading only in borderline cases. He evaluated journals "rather quickly," going through "bits and pieces" but not reading every entry.

Carl's History as a Writer and Teacher: Developing Expertise in Informing and Persuading His Audiences

Carl had learned from his professional writing experiences that he wrote best and most productively when he felt he was reaching and persuading his reader in ways he also tried to "get through" to his students. Carl's successful writing experiences outside academia led him to develop nontraditional goals for a university science educator. He nonetheless developed a fairly traditional understanding of the teacher's role in the introductory classroom.

Writing Carl "[hadn't] thought he could write" until, as a working professional, he was "writing all the time" and for meaningful communicative purposes he had been trained to address. As a high school and college student, Carl remembered having had "little encouragement" to write. His required freshman English course at Penn State was "difficult" and "a drudge" because he had "not [gotten] enough positive feedback to [believe] . . . I'm good at this or I want to do more of this."

If convinced he couldn't write for his composition teacher, Carl could write for himself, when there was nobody around to talk to. He remembered keeping a journal during periods of young adulthood when his life was in transition. One of them was the summer when he worked at the national park where he met his future wife:

> Just before going into the Navy, I spent the first part of the summer in Glacier Park. All I was doing was mopping, washing the dishes and the rest of the time was all mine. I had time to go out and sit under a tree in the shade and look up at the mountains and write in my journal . . . Thoreauvian-type things. One of my last entries is that I met this nurse who seemed real nice. And that's the last entry. No more sitting under the tree—at least alone.

When he enlisted in the Navy, Carl needed the journal again, briefly:

> For the first few days, I wrote in it every day. And then there was a couple of days when I wouldn't write, and then there was a week . . . then a month . . . now it's to the point where I write in it maybe once every ten years.

Journal writing had not sustained Carl's interest, but he worked productively on his master's thesis (a review and critique of selected research in palynology, the study of ancient plant spores). Carl's sense of competence and confidence in his writing ability improved with his thesis advisor's encouragement:

> This guy wasn't the type to . . . tell people they were good. . . . When he said, "You're not too bad a writer," boy that was

encouraging. I thought, "That's interesting, if I'm not too bad a writer."

As a working professional (an air pollution specialist with the Montana Department of Natural Resources), Carl was faced with an array of what he called "functional" writing tasks. He "sort of forgot . . . that [he] couldn't write" because he was "spending two or three hours a day" at it. Of the many letters, memos, and reports Carl wrote, his work on a report to a small town city manager on an impending street dust problem stood out. In working on it, he had struggled to reach and persuade his reader:

> I was thinking, what is it that you really want to say to this city manager out there in this small town. . . . Here I was . . . [writing] this report telling this person what they ought to be doing on their streets in their town. I had to write this in a way that they weren't going to just throw it . . . in the wastebasket. . . . I was really trying with all my might to tell them the story so they would accept it.

When Carl ultimately published this report as an article in *Public Works* magazine, he had experienced the evolution of a piece of writing in a process he would try to explain and illustrate when he assigned his "Spaceship Earth" students to write article reviews. At the D.N.R., Carl learned not only the value of writing, but the way writers in what he called the "real" world of professional activity needed to collaborate with one another and needed to understand and address interactions among various fields of endeavor. In the article Carl published in the UNI writing-across-the-curriculum newsletter, he introduced a call for required writing courses with reference to his professional writing experience ([Weber], 1984):

> Writing was of great importance in fulfilling the objectives of the governmental agency in which I worked. One of the requirements for employment there was the demonstration of writing ability, because poor writers put extra burdens on the rest of the staff as legal deadlines for our reports drew near. In addition to meeting legal deadlines, our reports had to be written in a way that clearly presented our analyses of how proposed engineering projects interacted with various economic, sociological, biological and geological components of the environment.

Carl went on to assert that "we should emphasize writing in our curriculum" to help students "obtain . . . employment and . . . do . . . a good job afterwards," and to "develop [their] understanding of course content as well as abilities in critical analysis." He reported that his article review and journal assignments in "Spaceship Earth" addressed these dual objectives. Journal keeping did this by giving "students practice in putting thoughts and ideas into writing," and by "creat[ing] a bridge" between students' own experiences, their reading of geological current events, and lecture and textbook material.

If Carl's experience as a journal writer had inclined him to understand journal keeping as personal writing, not meant to be shared with others, his professional writing experience suggested that journal keeping should be used to "create bridges."

Teaching After working for about ten years as an air pollution specialist and staff geologist for the Montana Department of Natural Resources, Carl decided in 1975 to return to The Pennsylvania State University for a doctorate. A new state administration had reduced his impact on environmental issues, and Carl thought he could "get through" to others more effectively as an educator.

Carl chose a doctoral program in which he could take education courses, but he pointed out that his D.Ed. in geology was "not an education degree" but a geology degree for prospective educators. Since his education courses had not taught him much about teaching—they "never really got into . . . what made a good teacher"—Carl felt he had learned "on the job" most of what he knew about teaching. He taught for two years at a small private college in Maine that "went under" and then took a job in 1982 at The University of Northern Iowa.

Carl's six years of university teaching experience inclined him to perceive a clear distinction between the content and teaching methods appropriate to his introductory courses—"Spaceship Earth" and a physical geology course for earth science majors—and his upper division environmental geology seminars. The seminars, enrolling 18 to 25 students, were discussion classes in which students were expected to negotiate meeting agendas with each other as well as their professor. (Students were assigned, for example, to work in teams on problems like those Carl had researched at the D.N.R., and they presented their findings in collaboratively produced reports.) On the other hand, in introductory classes like "Spaceship Earth," enrolling up to 75 students per section, Carl understood that he was expected to take primary responsibility for the agenda. Having found that University of Northern Iowa students were "polite . . . not intellectually slow, but passive," he understood that he had to "entertain them more" than his assertive Maine students.

There were several sources for Carl's expectation that, as the teacher of "Spaceship Earth," he needed to "entertain" his students. One of them was curricular: given the broad goals of the course (necessitated by its status as a general education offering), there never seemed to be enough time to involve students in much discussion; they needed to be informed about the basics of physical, historical, and environmental geology and then introduced to social and political aspects of geological processes and hazards. Even when time was created for discussion (as after the in-class writing on the light bulb), group size during the fall and spring semesters discouraged student-initiated interaction. (As Edwards & Furlong, 1978, point out, the more students in a group, the more risk any one of them typically takes in initiating communication with the teacher.)

Furthermore, the physical arrangement of the amphitheatre in which "Spaceship Earth" was conducted discouraged interaction among students and professor by dramatizing their separation with its rows of banked and bolted-down seats for the audience and podium for the lecturer. Carl's students entered this room expecting to be informed—and pleased to be entertained. When Carl entered the room, he was sometimes whistling, often ready with a joke, and always prepared to meet and exceed his students' expectations of his performance with easy-to-follow explanations, amusing stories, and vivid demonstrations. Their attentive looks, laughter, and appreciative comments fueled his enthusiasm for teaching, providing him with evidence, it seemed, that he was "getting through."

Although Carl's understanding of the teacher's role was fairly traditional, his professional experiences inclined him to develop nontraditional goals as a science educator. Five years before writing across the curriculum had become a goal at UNI, Carl came to teaching intending to incorporate in his science classes what he had learned from his professional experience about the value and process of writing. When the article critique and peer review sessions in "Spaceship Earth" turned out to be unsatisfactory, Carl retained the journal assignment; it reflected his ideology, and it supported the role to which he was accustomed as teacher of "Spaceship Earth."

Putting Ideology into Practice

Carl's ideas for undergraduate education encouraged him to become involved in two interrelated curricular reform projects at UNI, both of which influenced his teaching of "Spaceship Earth" and his assignment of journal keeping. His goals for the assignment reflect the humanistic ideology that he championed as a member of the university's general education committee, and the "expressivist" (Faigley, 1986) writing pedagogy he discovered in a university writing-across-the-curriculum workshop "justified" his hands-off approach to his students' journals.

When Carl came to the University of Northern Iowa in 1982, students were required to satisfy a university general education requirement by taking two or more credit hours from each of 12 categories of courses. According to program requirements approved in 1978, each of these categories was intended to provide "basic literacy in the fundamentals of human culture and knowledge." With such intentions, many of the categories overlapped: "Life and Its Interrelationships," "Environment, Technology and the Future" (the category for "Spaceship Earth"), and "Principles of the Physical Universe," for example, covered much of the same ground—at least on paper. Many of the courses assigned to satisfy general education requirements were introductory math, science, or humanities courses which, as taught, did not offer an interdisciplinary emphasis. Thus it had come as no surprise to the university administration when, in 1981, the North Central Association's accreditation report "faulted the institution," as the UNI provost reported in a letter to the faculty, "for 'lack of integration in the general education program.'" In 1983, Carl had volunteered to represent his college on the General Education Committee, charged the following year with overseeing, in Carl's words, "a better integrated and focused gen. ed. program." Three years later, the committee was ready to propose to the faculty senate a five-category program; Carl's ideas and language appear in the statement proposing a sequence of natural science courses, each intended to:

> develop an informed awareness of the interconnectedness of all aspects of the human and natural environments and the forces that operate in nature and society. Students should learn . . . that . . . the process of science is . . . conducted . . . by humans who live in societies largely governed by non-

scientific influences. The scientific enterprise is intimately connected to all other human activities.

When Carl worked on drafting this statement in 1984 and early 1985, unaware that "Spaceship Earth" would not be included in the final list of natural science courses, he revised its catalogue description so as "to emphasize that the course builds awareness of the interconnectedness between geologic processes and . . . social and political . . . aspects of experience." To further this objective, he assigned students to base "half of their journal entries . . . on articles [and] news items" so that "they [could] see [how] geology plays a fundamental and daily role in our society" ([Weber], 1984).

If Carl's involvement with general education planning had influenced his goals for the journal assignment, his participation in the university's (first) annual faculty workshop on writing across the curriculum provided him with a pedagogical basis for, in effect, giving students more leeway to make of the assignment what suited their interests. In his first two years of teaching the course, Carl had collected and read the journals, writing brief comments in some of them ("nice job!" or "source?"). He had found the job of collecting and reading over a hundred journals onerous, and commenting in them was not only time-consuming, but it also "went against the grain" of his understanding that journal writing was a "personal" activity. Thus he was interested to learn, at the WAC workshop in 1982, that writing theorists distinguished personal and expressive writing from writing for others, or transactional writing. Unlike transactional writing, expressive writing—journals, freewrites, and the like—did not need to be read or evaluated.

In the spring of 1985, Carl had not assigned journals, partly in response to students' complaints about the "Spaceship Earth" workload. When he decided to restore the assignment for the upcoming summer session (when course evaluations were not required), Carl defended his decision not to read or comment in students' journals with reference to the writing pedagogy offered in the WAC workshop:

> I have consciously made the decision that I didn't want to interfere in the journals. I didn't want to say something that would indicate to the student or make the student think that I was thinking this is right, this is wrong. I think I should stay out of the journals. I justify my laziness—or, I interpret

this on the basis of what . . . Toby Fulwiler . . . [said]: he said
a piano teacher doesn't have to sit and listen to a student
practice. You can assign writing without having to grade it
or even having to read it. . . . This is an assignment for them
to do for learning, not a grade, and certainly not my opinions on their opinions.

By telling students in his assignment directions that they were to
keep a "personal journal," written "for [them]selves," Carl hoped
to convey the message that this writing was intended for the kind
of unevaluated practice that writing theory supported. On the
other hand, he expected to hold students accountable for practicing as he intended them to—for drawing the connections he hoped
to see. By telling them he "might" read their journals "from time
to time," he could protect his interest in "staying out" of their
writing while sending them a message that they needed to be
keeping up. As the journals went uncollected and unread, however, students received the message they could use their journals
as they saw fit.

Managing the Class

Carl's choosing not to read or respond to his students' journals
had the effect of supporting the kind of class dynamics about
which he had complained. In one of the ironies that seem to
accompany the translation of ideology into pedagogy and pedagogy into classroom management, Carl's performance as a
teacher had the effect of encouraging students to use journals not
as he intended, but as they needed to use them. Although Carl's
expressed intention was for students to use journals to "illustrate
the connectedness" between their outside reading, their personal
experiences, and course topics, his students' appreciative responses to his enthusiastic performance made it seem more
expedient for him to "draw the connectedness" among personal,
social, and geological matters than to try to oblige them to do so
in their journals.

The more Carl lectured to his students, and the less they negotiated with him, the more likely they were to reflect if not reiterate his material in their journals and affirm his rhetoric and his
point of view. As students like Tina realized that their journals
would not be collected or read, most asked fewer questions, or
stopped asking them entirely: the less they used journals to raise

questions, the fewer questions they asked in class, encouraging Carl to lecture all the more.

When Carl tried, half-way through the semester, to use in-class journal writing as a prelude to discussion, his students were unaccustomed to trying out their own opinions in class, and no one ventured an opinion that deviated much from the interpretation hinted at in his introduction to the exercise. Although Carl preferred teaching "assertive" students who would raise questions and challenge his material, his domination of the agenda reduced the likelihood that challenges would be offered in class. If journal keeping—an opportunity for students to air their views—was assigned as an attempt to redress unequal "speaking rights," it served nonetheless to encourage Carl to lecture and to consolidate his authority. After all, this was what Carl's students, his superiors, and Carl himself as a professional academic were accustomed to expecting.

Addressing Institutional Expectations

The University of Northern Iowa had, historically, developed a reputation as a teaching institution. Founded as a normal school (in 1876), it invested heavily in a teacher education program to rival those offered by the other two Iowa regents' institutions, and its mission reflected a comprehensive commitment to "excellence in undergraduate education" (University of Northern Iowa, *Catalogue,* 1986–1987).

The journal assignment Carl made in the summer of 1986 represented what remained, in a sense, of the "idealistic" commitment to writing instruction with which Carl began his UNI career (when he had "thought [he] could solve America's educational problems . . . [with] writing assignments"). Although disturbed to see the "educational quality" of his class decline in the spring of 1986, when he suspended the article critique and essay exam, his career plans left him little choice.

After teaching a "fantastic" group of students in the summer of 1983, Carl decided in the fall of 1984 to supplement his article critique assignment with a required peer review of rough drafts. The critiques were not meeting his expectations: as he reported in "Writing Across the Curriculum is Not Enough," writers often missed the point of the articles they reviewed, plagiarized them, or summarized without analyzing or evaluating. However, the peer review sessions did not appear to make an appreciable difference in the quality of the final drafts. As Carl saw it, without preparation in critical writing or reading, his students were unprepared to make effective use of each other's responses. His feelings were echoed in several students' comments about the sessions in their journals: "It's obvious you really care about teaching," wrote a fall '84 "Spaceship Earth" student, "however I don't think students at this level are . . . mature enough to handle the peer criticism groups. Those in my group merely nodded after I read my paper and one girl got up and walked out." Another student "recommend[ed] dropping the workshop. We did this in my English class and I believe it's a good idea. However, the people in my group were very un-open in their critique of my paper. . . I don't think college age students should be forced to do such high school activities." Others complained more generally about the workload: "the research-type paper plus essay exams and a journal on top of that is excessive," or, simply, "too much writing for a gen. ed. class!"

In the spring and fall of 1984, complaints like these were registered in quantitative assessments that Carl's promotion advisory committee regarded as evidence of unsatisfactory teaching performance. On the ten-item evaluation questionnaire, Carl averaged a 3 (a *B*) on the six questions pertaining to his knowledge, skill, and accessibility as a teacher; on the four questions pertaining to Carl's evaluation procedures and his assignments, he averaged a 1.8. Many students praised Carl's "enthusiasm," his "concern for students," his sense of humor, and his "knowledge" in the space reserved for written comments, but the point totals fell below the 2.5 average that Carl understood he needed to produce.

Within two weeks of Carl's receipt of his promotion committee's report in early January, 1986, the university provost had sent a letter to all faculty urging adoption of the proposed new General Education Plan and support for

a policy amendment or new policy interpretation guidelines which would give special weight for excellence in general education instruction for tenure, promotion and merit salary increases. . . . The assessment data suggest that major courses are "better taught" (higher assessment scores) than general education courses even though we can all agree that our measuring instruments are imperfect.

Although Carl regarded it a "disaster for education when . . . evaluations are taken at face value" and it "didn't make [him] feel particularly good" to do so, in the 1986 spring semester he substituted the formerly required article critique with an optional extra-credit paper. He also decided not to assign journal keeping. His evaluations improved, as he predicted they would (averaging a 3.2), but the class was one of the "dullest" he had taught, and students' "passivity" in class "depressed [his] ability." Attributing this passivity, in part, to students' failure to engage in thinking or writing about the class, and aware that he would not be required to submit evaluations for his summer class, he was prepared to restore the journal assignment.

An Effective Compromise?

At the end of the summer '86 session, Carl had mixed reactions to journal keeping in his class. He recognized that, by not reading the journals, he had encouraged some students to disregard his intentions. His pedagogical basis for taking a hands-off approach was not entirely convincing—perhaps it simply "justified his laziness." On the other hand, the journals provided evidence that all the writers were "doing at least a little bit of thinking," and that some, like Beth, were making the "personal connections" that he had hoped to see. Others, by summarizing readings (or worse, class notes), were not doing the kind of reflecting or questioning that he expected, and he decided to try to discourage future classes from using journals as study guides. (His discouragement would take the form of his telling students not to use them that way.) Otherwise, he had no plans to alter the course or the assignment.

6

A POSTSCRIPT AND SOME CONCLUDING OBSERVATIONS

Postscript

From the standpoint of Carl's career plans, reducing his once ambitious writing agenda to the journal assignment did not appear, in the spring of 1987, to have made the difference he hoped it would. His student evaluation point totals rose above the 2.5 mark, and a departmental promotion committee voted to grant him tenure in early March, 1987. Carl's application was nonetheless denied by the dean of his college on the grounds that Carl hadn't published enough. Carl applied for and received a summer research grant in 1987, had two articles accepted for publication that fall, and was granted tenure in the spring of 1988.

Carl had guessed correctly that "Spaceship Earth" might not be a part of the new university general education program, slated to go into effect in the fall of 1989. In the fall of 1988, Carl planned to teach the course for his seventeenth and last time. With Carl's support, his colleagues on the earth science and general education curriculum committees decided that "Spaceship Earth" overlapped with existing physical and environmental geology courses, and that the interdisciplinary emphasis of the course was better represented in the physics department's general education offering called "Environment, Technology, and Society." At his request, Carl Weber was assigned to develop and teach a new earth science general education course to be called "Life Through Time." He anticipated that this course, emphasizing "living systems throughout history," would be structured and taught much like its predecessor, "Spaceship Earth."

In his first years of teaching "Spaceship Earth," Carl had intended the journal keeping to support—he called it a "prelude" to—the article critique, peer review, and essay exams. These writing assignments succumbed to the curricular and institutional pressures described in the previous chapter. However, Carl's intentions for writing would be vindicated in 1987, when the university faculty senate approved a writing-across-the-curriculum program as part of the new general education package. This new curricular initiative would replace an exit writing competency exam with the freshman course Carl had called for in 1984 (in "Writing Across the Curriculum is Not Enough"). Furthermore, academic departments would be required to determine what constituted writing competency in their fields and provide students with "appropriate" writing experiences. Carl's colleagues would be obliged to find ways to give their students the kind of writing practice Carl had advocated.

In December of 1987, Tina graduated from The University of Northern Iowa with high honors—a 3.65 cumulative average—and a 3.7 average in her physics major. She took a job at Minnesota Laser, a Minneapolis-based electronics firm.

By December 1987, Beth had also left the university. True to her description of herself as an "on-again, off-again" college student, she withdrew from UNI in the fall semester of 1986.

Concluding Observations

The story of writing in "Spaceship Earth" raises a number of questions about journal keeping, about the uses for writing assignments in university classes like this one, and about the role that writing can play in courses across the curriculum. I began the study which generated this account expecting that "Spaceship Earth" students would use their journals to make the connections among personal, social, and geological issues that Professor Weber said he wanted this assignment to encourage. I found instead that Weber's students used journals to prepare for and comment on class activities, recount their teacher's lectures, or summarize their reading. I also expected that Professor Weber, an enthusiastic advocate of writing across the curriculum, would make journal keeping a regular and visible part of the life of his class. He had come to teach at UNI with the idea that students needed to be doing more and different kinds of writing if they were to make the best of their university experience and were to be adequately prepared for professional careers. But by the summer of 1986, for curricular and institutional as well as personal reasons, Weber had chosen to give less time and energy to writing assignments than to other more traditional classroom activities like lecturing and multiple-choice testing, and to refer to the journals in class only rarely.

What are we to make of these discrepancies between Weber's original hopes and plans for writing in "Spaceship Earth," and the uses that he and his students ended up making of journal keeping? Did Weber misunderstand, and have we misunderstood, how journals work? I have suggested that social, curricular, and institutional expectations of university teachers' and students' behaviors are shaping forces in the design and management of academic writing assignments. How can writing assignments work, then, to facilitate learning across the curriculum?

There are also questions about the way I have developed and presented this account. To my research question, "what are journals used for?" I have offered answers drawn from the personal histories and experiences of my informants, as well as from the academic and institutional setting in which they interacted. What justifies my collecting biographical information that is temporally and physically outside the immediate classroom context for journal keeping in "Spaceship Earth"? I have also gone to unusual lengths in Chapter 2 to account for the role my own experiences and expectations played in the research process. Why have I bothered trying to make the activities of research a central part of the account of what was studied? I will address these questions with a few concluding observations about journal keeping as an academic assignment, writing as a tool for learning across the curriculum, and reflexivity in ethnographic methodology.

Journal Keeping as an Academic Assignment   I pointed out in Chapter 1 that journal keeping is widely understood to promote intellectual growth and provide opportunity for the decentralizing of traditionally teacher-centered classroom authority (Fulwiler, 1987). The account I have presented suggests that the effects journal keeping may have on students' learning and on the class agenda and dynamics are closely tied to the way the assignment is designed and presented, the way it is responded to, and the way it is related to other assignments and activities. Although Weber told the class when he introduced the assignment that he expected them to write regularly and reflectively on connections among their own and course-related issues, he subsequently chose not to provide them with much incentive to do so. By choosing not to read or respond to his students' journals, he encouraged them to use the assignment not as he first asked them to, but as it would serve their own best interests as students in the class.

These interests were shaped, in part, by the way the course was designed and the class was managed. Weber gave his students multiple-choice tests based on lectures and textbook material—and not on the kinds of connections he had asked for in the journals. Thus he implicitly encouraged students to use their journals not as places to reflect on out-of-class reading, but as study guides in which to review potential test material. By using most of the class time for lecture and demonstration—and not obliging students to contribute their own experiences or reading to the agenda—Weber reduced the likelihood that students would reflect on personal experiences relevant to geological current events in their journals. Although Weber called for challenges or complaints, he presented information in class with such authority that journal keepers tended to discount or hedge any reservations about their teacher's material, as he predicted they would when he made the journal assignment. (He had predicted that negative comments would be "balanced" with praise.) Although Tina, Beth, and their classmates responded to what they took to be their professor's expectations of their journals, their incentives to write reflectively, expansively, or critically on connections among their own and course-related issues weakened in the absence of reinforcement from Weber.

Discrepancies between Weber's stated intentions for the assignment and the uses he and his students made of it cannot simply be traced to Weber's handling of the class or the assignment; this account also suggests that students' and teachers' uses for writing are shaped by their individual histories, their expectations, and their out-of-class roles and responsibilities. By collecting information about my informants' past experiences, I learned that their approaches to journal keeping in "Spaceship Earth" in many ways resembled their approaches to previous academic writing and journal keeping activities. For example, Beth used in her journal the imagination and questioning intelligence that had won over the readers of her papers in college literature classes; and Tina deployed the knowledge of science and skill at exposition that had earned her *As* on most of the school-sponsored writing she had done. Their experiences as journal keepers shaped their attitudes toward the "Spaceship Earth" journal as well as their strategies in negotiating this open-ended assignment. For example, Beth tended to avoid doing the writing because earlier journal keeping for teachers had required uncomfortable self-disclosure. Tina chose to write summaries as she had in a journal kept for an introductory college physics course. This time Tina enjoyed the summarizing because she could choose the material.

Carl Weber was not inclined to read or respond to his students' journals because his own journal keeping experience had been private; he had kept a journal as a substitute for needed communication with others. He had lost interest in journal keeping because, so far as I could ascertain, he had not used his journal in connection with developing or communicating his ideas to others. It had, briefly, displaced the give-and-take with others that he needed. An important reason for Weber's disappointment with many of his students' journals—disappointment that he discounted by giving all but one of them credit anyway—was his failure to consider the relevance of his own experience of journal keeping to the experience his students might be likely to have. That he ignored his own personal disinclination to keep a journal when he made this assignment is somewhat puzzling. In teaching, Weber often told stories that communicated the message that people who failed to learn from past experience were asking for trouble. Why, then, did he choose not to read or respond to his students' journals when his own private and unshared journal writing had petered out?

One answer is that the 1982 UNI Writing-Across-the-Curriculum Workshop Weber had attended had encouraged him to distinguish personal and expressive writing from writing for others. The workshop leaders (of whom I was one) followed composition theoreticians in making what I now think is a reductive distinction between expressive and transactional writing. The distinction appeared to be sensible for several reasons. For one thing, the texts of journal entries display a self-referring rhetoric that often looks to be unmediated by awareness of an audience. For another, journal keepers, asked about their intentions, tend to confirm their teachers' reasons for assigning them to keep journals; they say that they use journals to express or rehearse their own opinions. The UNI workshop leader emphasized that students' journals need not be shared or responded to, unaware that even when writing is not used explicitly as a medium of communication, writers negotiate their rhetoric and meanings with social and political intentions. Thus Weber did not predict that many of his students would find it just as difficult as he had to sustain a thoughtful, reflective, or, as he put it, "Thoreauvian" rhetoric in the absence of an interested and encouraging reader.

Personal and outside-of-class experience was one important shaping force in journal keeping. Role relationships between students and teacher and the dynamics of interaction in class were no less important to the way class participants construed the assignment. As people who wanted to learn about geology, "Spaceship Earth" students probably expected to use their journals to help them better understand geological issues. As students in a particular kind of college class, responding to a particular kind of teacher, however, Beth, Tina, and their classmates also used writing, as they used talk and other social behaviors, to help them develop and earn credit for relationships with classmates and teacher. They used writing to help them develop their authority as students as Weber used it to develop his as their instructor. If Weber, as an educator, understood that journal keeping could be used to help students take more responsibility for the class agenda, he found, as a teacher, that students seemed to expect him to take primary responsibility. Altering the role the assignment played in the course would have necessitated altering a role with which he was comfortable as teacher of the course. Making the journals occasions for discussion would have obliged him to construe his authority as teacher of "Spaceship Earth" differently. It would have required that he relinquish some of the control he exercised over the syllabus and offer for negotiation material that he, his students, and his superiors regarded as nonnegotiable.

Writing as an Academic Learning Tool The story of writing in "Spaceship Earth" suggests that writing across the curriculum is not enough to "solve educational problems," as Carl Weber had predicted. A journal, a peer critique workshop, or an essay exam are not likely to encourage students to write more reflectively or behave more assertively in class if they are not otherwise finding incentives to negotiate the agenda for learning. The teacher's role, the physical organization of the classroom, the procedures for evaluation of students' performance, class size, and students' and teachers' backgrounds and expectations are among the many contexts for classroom learning that send messages about what can be said and written.

The "Spaceship Earth" story suggests to me that one of the most important and problematic of these contexts is the curricular setting for course goals and plans. In a general education course like "Spaceship Earth," with broad, preordained and, to my mind, conflicting goals, students and faculty lack the incentives to negotiate the agenda that they find in upper-division courses with more focused objectives. Despite published statements that "Spaceship Earth" emphasized the social and political relevance of geological issues, an equally if not more important agenda for the course was instruction in basic geological literacy. Weber often referred to a difference between "academic" geology—terms, categories, or theoretical premises of the sort his students were primarily tested on—and the "real world" geology that is concerned with where to build homes, bury toxic wastes, or find strategic metals outside South Africa. These are the sorts of issues that "drew the connectedness" which the students were asked to consider in their journals. Given the basic literacy emphasis of multiple-choice exams, necessitated by curricular expectations and typical class size, many students used writing to master terms and concepts, leaving their enthusiastic instructor to draw real-world connections for them. After all, it was really the purpose of the upper-division environmental seminar—and not "Spaceship Earth"—to involve class participants in making the kinds of connections and decisions that writing assignments like an article critique, a peer review, an essay exam, or a journal would facilitate.

This account raises some difficult questions about the role writing can play in university curriculum programs of general education. To my mind, however nobly humanistic their stated goals may be, such programs are nonetheless intended to serve the academy's political and economic needs by extending the territory of college into two preparatory years before the two years of focused disciplinary and preprofessional course work. Designed to enroll the maximum number of students at minimum cost to the institution, general education courses work as academic socialization programs that typically dramatize role and status differences among students and professors, differences that encourage professors to lecture and students to sit quietly and take notes. Like talk and other classroom behaviors, writing in such courses inescapably highlights these differences, supporting the kinds of rote learning that large class size, quantitative exams, and bloated syllabi encourage.

At the beginning of this account, I suggested that writing-across-the-curriculum ideology and practice is divided on the issue of the roles writing can or should play in university curricula. Given the forces of institutional and curricular expectation, is there any hope for practical application of claims that writing, as a mode of knowing and learning, deserves a fundamental place in the curriculum? Clearly, writing itself does not democratize classrooms; people do. As writing-across-the-curriculum programs mature, it remains to be seen how much power writing will have to facilitate change in roles and relationships in which students, faculty, and administrators seem deeply entrenched.

In the writing-across-the-curriculum movement, those who assume writing should serve academic and disciplinary purposes now seem (at least in the professional forums) to be in ascendancy over the idealists, for whom writing is ultimately nothing less than a force for radical curricular change. It is interesting that the academic discourse pragmatists have come to the forefront of composition studies during an era in which conservatism has dominated the larger scene of American political life. This connection suggests to me that the ideologies and practices of composition studies are tossed by nonacademic cultural and political forces that reach into and through writing as an academic discipline. In accounts like this one, we can begin to try to locate these forces and interpret their influence.

Reflexivity in Ethnographic Methodology   As I pointed out in Chapter 2, this account differs from other ethnographies in composition in its emphasis on my role in the study. By describing how research activities evolved in negotiation with my informants, whose expectations and interests influenced and were influenced by my own, I have tried to suggest that the process of investigation and its outcomes are interrelated and reflexive activities. Other ethnographers in composition have assumed that written texts represent social and cultural awareness, and they indicate that they participated in as well as observed the social world of the texts they interpret. (See, for example, Doheny-Farina, 1984; Dyson, 1985; Florio & Clark, 1982.) But ethnographic narratives like Florio and Clark's, Dyson's, or Doheny-Farina's stop short of accounting for the ways their participation affected the world of the study. Ethnographies that do not acknowledge the researcher's role may risk jeopardizing the credibility of their interpretations. (For example, as I suggested in Chapter 1, evidence of Florio and Clark's unacknowledged influence on research subjects, in the form of a child's love note, points to other uses for writing than those they delineate.)

As a type of narrative, any ethnographic account, no matter how objective or subjective, attempts to tell a coherent and persuasive story: point of view is one of many rhetorical strategies available to the narrator, some drawn from social science research conventions, some from nonfiction reporting, some from the plot and characterization devices associated with fiction. Traditionally, ethnographic narratives distinguish the story of the research subjects from the researcher's story, which may never get told. But as a means of incorporating diverse rhetorical stances in one coherent whole, reflexivity suggests possibilities for the revising of this tradition, and the creation of new kinds of ethnographic texts. In this text, elaboration of the observer's point of view points the way, perhaps, toward a more explicit continuity between methodology and outcomes, observer and observed. We can never fully account for the origins of our research, but we can make interpretation more comprehensive when we address its social evolution.

Bartholomae, D. (1985). Inventing the university. In M. Rose (Ed.), *When a writer can't write* (pp. 134–165). New York: Guilford.

Basso, K. (1974). The ethnography of writing. In R. Bauman & J. Sherzer (Eds.), *The ethnography of speaking* (pp. 425–432). Cambridge, UK: Cambridge University Press.

Bazerman, C. (1983). Scientific writing as a social act: A review of the literature of the sociology of science. In P. V. Anderson, R. J. Brockmann, & C. R. Miller (Eds.), *New essays in technical and scientific communication: Research, theory, practice* (pp. 156–184). Farmingdale, NY: Baywood.

Berthoff, A. E. (1981). *The making of meaning: Metaphors, models, and maxims for writing teachers.* Upper Montclair, NJ: Boynton/Cook.

Bizzell, P. (1982). Cognition, convention, and certainty: What we need to know about writing. *PRE/TEXT, 3,* 213–243.

Bogdan, R., & S. J. Taylor. (1984). *Introduction to qualitative research methods: The search for meanings* (2nd ed.). New York: Wiley.

Brandt, D. (1986). Toward an understanding of context in composition. *Written Communication, 3,* 139–157.

Britton, J., Burgess, T., Martin, N., McLeod, A., & Rosen, H. (1975). *The development of writing abilities (11–18).* London: Schools Council Publications.

Brodkey, L. (1987). *Academic writing as a social practice.* Philadelphia: Temple University Press.

Bruffee, K. A. (1978). The Brooklyn plan: Attaining intellectual growth through peer-group tutoring. *Liberal Education, 64,* 447–469.

Bruffee, K. A. (1984). Collaborative learning and the "conversation of mankind." *College English, 46,* 635–652.

Cooper, M. (1986). The ecology of writing. *College English, 48,* 364–373.

Culler, J. (1981). *The pursuit of signs*. Ithaca, NY: Cornell University Press.

Damage in Mexico: A double quake. (1986, January 11). *Science News*, p. 25.

Delamont, S. (1983). *Interaction in the classroom* (2nd ed.). London: Methuen.

Doheny-Farina, S. (1984). *Writing in an emergent business organization: An ethnographic study*. Unpublished doctoral dissertation, Rensselaer Polytechnic Institution.

Doheny-Farina, S. (1986). Writing in an emerging organization: An ethnographic study. *Written Communication, 3,* 158–185.

Dorsey, C. K. (1985). *Journal writing: Its effects on the development of syntactic maturity and attitude in students' writing*. Unpublished doctoral dissertation, The University of Tennessee.

Dyson, A. H. (1984). Learning to write/learning to do school: Emergent writers' interpretations of school literacy tasks. *Research in the Teaching of English, 18,* 233–264.

Dyson, A. H. (1985). Second graders sharing writing: The multiple social realities of a literacy event. *Written Communication, 2,* 189–215.

Edwards, A. D., & Furlong, V. J. (1978). *The language of teaching: Meaning in classroom interaction*. London: Heinemann.

Elbow, P. (1981). *Writing with power*. New York: Oxford University Press.

Emig, J. (1977). Writing as a mode of learning. *College Composition and Communication, 28,* 122–128.

Faigley, L. (1986). Competing theories of process: A critique and a proposal. *College English, 48,* 527–542.

Faigley, L., & Hansen, K. (1985). Learning to write in the social sciences. *College Composition and Communication, 36,* 140–149.

Fishman, A. R. (1984). *Reading, writing, and meaning: A literacy study among the Amish*. Unpublished doctoral dissertation, University of Pennsylvania.

Florio, S., & Clark, C. (1982). The functions of writing in an elementary classroom. *Research in the Teaching of English, 16,* 115–130.

Fulwiler, T. (1980). Journals across the disciplines. *English Journal, 69*, 14–19.

Fulwiler, T. (1982). The personal connection: Journal writing across the curriculum. In T. Fulwiler & A. Young (Eds.), *Language connections: Writing and reading across the curriculum* (pp. 15–31). Urbana, IL: National Council of Teachers of English.

Fulwiler, T. (1986). The argument for writing across the curriculum. In A. Young & T. Fulwiler (Eds.), *Writing across the disciplines: Research into practice* (pp. 21–32). Upper Montclair, NJ: Boynton/Cook.

Fulwiler, T. (Ed.). (1987). *The journal book.* Upper Montclair, NJ: Boynton/Cook.

Geertz, C. (1973). *The interpretation of cultures.* New York: Basic Books.

Geertz, C. (1983). *Local knowledge: Further essays in interpretive anthropology.* New York: Basic Books.

Goetz, J., & LeCompte, M. (1984). *Ethnography and qualitative design in educational research.* Orlando, FL: Academic Press.

Grice, H. P. (1975). Logic and conversation. In P. Cole & J. Morgan (Eds.), *Syntax and semantics, vol. 3: Speech acts* (pp. 41–58). New York: Academic Press.

Hallberg, F. (1987). Journal writing as person making. In T. Fulwiler (Ed.), *The journal book* (pp. 289–305). Upper Montclair, NJ: Boynton/Cook.

Hammersley, M. (1983). *The ethnography of schooling: Methodological issues.* Driffield, UK: Nafferton Books.

Hargreaves, D. H. (1972). *Interpersonal relations and education.* London: Routledge and Kegan Paul.

Harris, J. (1986). The role of expressive discourse in the teaching of writing: A review of current composition texts. *Freshman English News, 15*, 2–8.

Healy, M. K. (1984). *Writing in a science class: A case study of the connections between writing and learning.* Unpublished doctoral dissertation, New York University.

Heath, S. B. (1983). *Ways with words: Language, life, and work in communities and classrooms.* New York: Cambridge University Press.

Herrington, A. J. (1985). Writing in academic settings: A study of the contexts for writing in two college chemical engineering courses. *Research in the Teaching of English, 19,* 330–359.

Jensen, V. (1987). Writing in college physics. In T. Fulwiler (Ed.), *The journal book* (pp. 330–336). Upper Montclair, NJ: Boynton/Cook.

Jolliffe, D. (1984). *Audience, subject, form, and ways of speaking: Writers' knowledge in the disciplines.* Unpublished doctoral dissertation, University of Texas, Austin.

Knoblauch, C. H., & Brannon, L. (1983). Writing as learning through the curriculum. *College English, 45,* 465–474.

Leahy, R. (1985). The power of the three student journal. *College Teaching, 33,* 108–112.

Long, M. (1980). Inside the 'black box': Methodological issues in classroom research on language learning. *Language Learning, 30,* 1–42.

Macrorie, K. (1976). *Telling writing* (2nd ed.). Rochelle Park, NJ: Hayden.

Making a date with light (1985, February 9). *Science News,* p. 88

Marshall, J. (1984). Process and product: Case studies of writing in two content areas. In A. N. Applebee (Ed.), *Contexts for learning to write: Studies of secondary school instruction* (pp. 149–168). Norwood, NJ: Ablex Publishing Corp.

McCarthy, L. (1985). *A stranger in strange lands: A college student writing across the curriculum.* Unpublished doctoral dissertation, University of Pennsylvania.

Montgomery, C. (1986). *Environmental geology.* Dubuque, IA: William C. Brown.

North, S. (1985). Journal writing across the curriculum: A reconsideration. *Freshman English News, 14*(2), 2–9.

North, S. (1986a). Writing in a philosophy class: Three case studies. *Research in the Teaching of English, 20,* 160–197.

North, S. (1986b). *Research on expressive writing: A problem of definition.* Paper presented at 37th Annual Meeting, Conference on College Composition and Communication, New Orleans, LA.

North, S. (1987). *The making of knowledge in composition: Portrait of an emerging field.* Upper Montclair, NJ: Boynton/Cook.

Odell, L. (1985). Beyond the text: Relations between writing and social context. In L. Odell & D. Goswami (Eds.), *Writing in nonacademic settings* (pp. 249–280). New York: Guilford.

Odell, L., & Goswami, D. (1982). Writing in a nonacademic setting. *Research in the Teaching of English, 16,* 201–223.

Parker, R. P., & Goodkin, V. (1987). *The consequences of writing: Enhancing learning in the disciplines.* Upper Montclair, NJ: Boynton/Cook.

Perelman, L. (1986). The context of classroom writing. *College English, 48,* 471–479.

Porter, J. (1986). Intertextuality and the discourse community. *Rhetoric Review, 5,* 34–45.

Pratt, M. L. (1977). *Toward a speech act theory of literary discourse.* Bloomington, IN: Indiana University Press.

Progoff, I. (1975). *At a journal workshop: The basic text and guide for using the intensive journal.* New York: Dialogue House Library.

Progoff, I. (1983). *Life study: Experiencing creative lives through the intensive journal method.* New York: Dialogue House Library.

Reece, S. (1981). *The journal keeps the person in the process.* (ERIC Document Reproduction Service No. ED 193 665)

Robinson, P. (1981). *Perspectives on the sociology of education: An introduction.* London: Routledge and Kegan Paul.

Robinson-Metz, J. M. (1985). *Case studies of the journal writing process. Three eleventh grade journal writers.* Unpublished doctoral dissertation, New York University.

Rohmann, D. G. (1965). Prewriting: The stage of discovery in the writing process. *College Composition and Communication, 16,* 106–112.

Scribner, S., & Cole, M. (1981). Unpackaging literacy. In M. F. Whiteman (Ed.), *Writing: The nature, development, and teaching of written communication, vol. 1: Functional and linguistic-cultural differences* (pp. 71–87). Hillsdale, NJ: Erlbaum.

Selfe, C., & Arbabi, F. (1986). Writing to learn: Engineering student journals. In A. Young & T. Fulwiler (Eds.), *Writing across the disciplines: Research into practice* (pp. 184–191). Upper Montclair, NJ: Boynton/Cook.

Staton, J., Shuy, R., & Kreeft, J. R. (1982). *Analysis of dialogue journal writing as a communicative event.* Final report to the National Institute of Education (ERIC Document Reproduction Service No. ED 214 196).

Stubbs, M. (1983). *Language, schools, and classrooms* (2nd ed.). New York: Methuen.

Swanson-Owens, D. (1986). Identifying natural sources of resistance: A case study of implementing writing across the curriculum. *Research in the Teaching of English, 20,* 68–97.

Tierney, R. (1981). Using expressive writing to teach biology. In A. Wotring & R. Tierney, *Two studies of writing in high school science* (pp. 47–83). Berkeley, CA: Bay Area Writing Project.

University of Northern Iowa. (1986). *Catalogue, 1986–1987.* Cedar Falls, IA: University of Northern Iowa.

Walters, S. A., & Weiss, R. (1979). *Research on writing and learning: Some effects of learning-centered writing in five subject areas.* (ERIC Document Reproduction Service No. ED 191 073)

[Weber, C.] (1984). Writing across the curriculum is not enough. *Toward Better Writing, 1,* 5–6. (Newsletter of the Writing Center, Center for Academic Achievement, University of Northern Iowa.)

Yinger, R. J., & Clark, C. M. (1981). *Reflective journal writing: Theory and practice.* Occasional Paper No. 50, Institute for Research on Teaching, College of Education, Michigan State University, East Lansing, MI.

Young, A., & Fulwiler, T. (Eds.). (1986). *Writing across the disciplines: Research into practice.* Upper Montclair, NJ: Boynton/ Cook.